What is a railway?

It seems to me as if this railway were one typical achievement of the age in which we live, as if it brought together in one plot all the ends of the world and all the degrees of social rank.

Robert Louis Stevenson, The Amateur Emigrant, 1879

THE railway was the greatest and the most profoundly influential technical development of the nineteenth century. With its combination of power and speed the railway enabled large quantities of goods and people to be transported from one place to another in a short time, and so influenced and in some way changed the lives of all – from the monarch to the humblest artisan.

The typical dictionary definition of a railway (a set of iron rails for the passage of trains and cars or trucks drawn by a locomotive engine and conveying passengers and goods) does little to extol a system of transport that combines the best of contemporary developments in science and technology with considerable romance.

The railways began life as an industrial transport system. The application of steam power revolutionised their scope until the remotest settlements heard the rhythm. As steam became outmoded, internal combustion were experimented with and contemporary materials. They systems of operational and financial control and gained for themselves a good safety record.

Above all, railways are about people – the engineers and technicians who devise the schemes and apply the technology; the entrepreneurs who supply the finance; and the people who use the systems. The concept of mass mobility grew with the railways. People used the railways to go to work, to travel for pleasure and to service new industries. Towns were developed as centres of the railway industry; suburbs grew and newly rail-connected seaside resorts flourished. In countries large and small the railways helped to bring about the regulation of life by the standardisation of time. Fresh food and vegetables carried by train became widely available. Mail and newspapers were sent rapidly from one part of the country to another. Large quantities of raw materials and finished goods could be transported to factories and shops.

For over a hundred years the railways were the pre-eminent form of land transport. The displays at the National Railway Museum bear witness to that supremacy and bring together a unique blend of science, technology and social development.

Waterloo station, 1946

The permanent way

THE main characteristic of a railway, as its name implies, is the prepared track or system of rails on which the railway vehicles run. A smooth wheel on a smooth rail minimises the friction between the two and reduces the effort required to move heavy loads. The carefully designed profiles of the flanged railway wheels and of the rail-heads ensure that vehicles are self-steering along the tracks.

The earliest railways were grooved stone wagon ways used by the Greeks and Romans. Railways, using wooden rails, existed in European mines from the sixteenth century and later further afield. People and horses were used to push or pull the trucks along. It was not, however, until the development of the steam locomotive in Britain, early in the nineteenth century, that the advantages of the railway system, in particular speed and the ability to move greater loads, could be fully exploited and adopted by the world. The early 'L'-shaped plateway rails, which had proved satisfactory while horses or men provided the motive power, were too flimsy for use with heavy steam locomotives. Edge rails, many early examples of which were 'fish-bellied', with a thicker centre section to give strength to the rail, proved moderately successful but were still brittle and liable to break. By 1820 the technique of rolling wrought-iron rails in 20 feet lengths had been perfected. Wrought iron was much less brittle than cast iron and therefore better able to support the weight of steam locomotives. Steel rails, up to 60 times more resilient than wrought iron, were introduced in 1857 by the Midland Railway. Laid on wooden sleepers and kept in well-drained alignment by a bed of stone chip ballast, the permanent way had achieved the form it was to retain for many years.

At first glance, modern track looks very similar to that used in the age of steam. There are, however, significant differences. The sleepers are now of concrete or steel and the rail of a profile called 'flat-bottom', sitting directly on the sleeper and held in place by a tensile steel clip. On sections of track which are free of points the rails are welded into lengths of up to a mile. The rails are pre-stressed when laid, in order to overcome the effects of change in temperature, and have sliding expansion joints at intervals. The rails themselves are insulated from their sleepers and fastenings as they carry a weak electrical current to assist signalling. This system is called 'track circuiting' and is explained in the section on 'safety and signalling', p.16.

The condition of the railway track is very important for the safe and regular operation of train services. It is vital that the track is well maintained and regularly inspected. For example, the track gauge or distance between the rail centres, in Britain 4ft 8½ins, must be correct; the ballast must support the sleepers properly; the surrounding area must be kept clear of vegetation and other obstacles. Track maintenance is carried out regularly by gangs of platelayers who can often be seen working on the line.

Iron plate rails laid on stone sleeper blocks on the Little Eaton tramway, Derbyshire c 1900

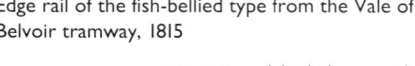
Edge rail of the fish-bellied type from the Vale of Belvoir tramway, 1815

Stockton & Darlington Railway boundary marker, 1825

Replica of a medieval mining truck on primitive rails as used in the mines of Central Europe

The Permanent Way – Relaying, by Stanhope Forbes, a poster design for the London Midland & Scottish Railway, 1924

Great Western Railway handcrane No 537 of 1899, on bull-head steel rails. The crane was used for permanent way work until 1977

Continuous steel welded rail with Thermit welding kit, 1992

Permanent way gang working at Bolton station in 1914

Things to see ...

The Great Hall

The first rails
A replica of a medieval mining truck stands on primitive rails as used in Germany in the sixteenth century. Note the guiding pin between the wheels.

Cast-iron rails
This display shows the frame of a Belvoir Castle truck and edge rail of the 'fish-bellied' type from the Vale of Belvoir tramway, 1815.

Steel rails
The section of steel rail track has a Great Western Railway hand crane of 1899 standing on it. Notice the components of the track: the ballast, wooden sleepers, cast iron chairs and keys to hold the bull-head rail in position.

Continuous steel welded rail
The display shows three types of sleeper and the Pandrol clips holding the rail in position. A Thermit welding kit indicates where the rails are welded together to form continuous track.

The development of the locomotive
Steam traction

THE introduction to the railway of the steam locomotive was to unlock its potential as a transport system. For 25 years the locomotive's performance was limited by its design, which was that of a mobile beam engine. Then in 1829 new features appeared in a locomotive called *Rocket* which increased the power and speed of the engine relative to its weight and so revolutionised rail travel.

The driving mechanism of *Rocket* was direct from the cylinders and pistons to the wheels

A steam locomotive uses steam under pressure to operate. Steam from the locomotive boiler passes into the cylinders where, by means of the valve gear, it moves the pistons backwards and forwards. The pistons are joined to connecting rods which through a system of cranks turn the wheels. Richard Trevithick designed the world's first steam railway locomotive. It ran at Pen-y-darren, South Wales, on 21 February 1804. Other engineers, recognising its potential, designed a number of similar locomotives which were basically mobile beam engines, heavy and slow but capable of pulling several loaded wagons from mine to river or canal. *Agenoria*, built in 1829, marks the end of this line of development.

In 1829 the 'modern' steam locomotive appeared. *Rocket*, designed by Robert Stephenson and Henry Booth, won the Liverpool & Manchester Railway's locomotive trials at Rainhill, Lancashire. *Rocket* embodied many new features which were to become standard for all steam locomotives. In the boiler, hot gases from the burning coke in the firebox were drawn through 25 small tubes surrounded by water. The drawing action was assisted by the blast of the exhaust steam from the cylinders, which was passed up the chimney. *Rocket's* firebox was also surrounded by water. These arrangements helped to boil water more rapidly, which made faster running possible. Another innovation was direct drive from the cylinders and pistons to the wheels, which eliminated the need for the complicated gears and levers of earlier locomotives. *Rocket* marked a turning point in the development of the locomotive. By 1833 the steam locomotive had acquired its characteristic form. The firebox, boiler and smokebox were mounted on frames that supported the cylinders. Large wheels drove the locomotive, smaller idle wheels supported the weight and provided a smoother entry into curved track. A tender carried coke and water.

Distinct types of locomotives, for goods and passenger duties, were soon designed. Passenger locomotives had large driving wheels so that they could run fast. Great Northern Railway locomotive No 1 (1870), the Stirling single with 8ft driving wheels, is a classic example. Locomotives were also designed with coupled driving wheels to combine speed with better adhesion. The 4-4-0 locomotive with a leading bogie and four driving wheels dominated express passenger train operation in Britain in the late nineteenth and early twentieth centuries: North Eastern Railway No 1621 (1893), London & South Western Railway No 563 (1893) and South Eastern & Chatham Railway No 737 (1901) are notable examples. The 4-4-2 locomotive (Great Northern Railway No 251 (1902) is an example) allowed for a larger firebox and ashpan supported by the trailing axle than was possible with the 4-4-0 or 4-6-0 design, and thus improved steaming.

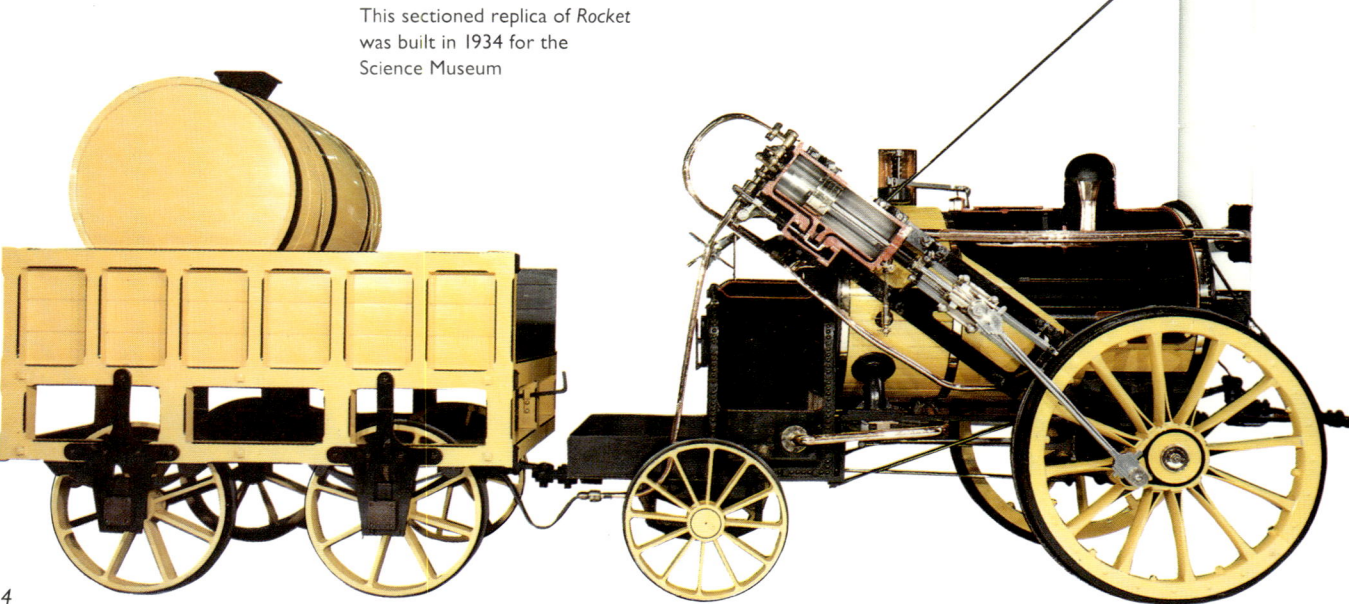

This sectioned replica of *Rocket* was built in 1934 for the Science Museum

The 0-4-0 goods locomotive *Agenoria* built in 1829 worked at the Shutt End Colliery in Staffordshire for over 30 years

Things to see ...

The Great Hall
0-4-0 goods locomotive *Agenoria* (1829)
Agenoria is a contemporary of *Rocket*, winner of the Rainhill Locomotive Trials in 1829, but is of a much earlier design. It is basically a mobile beam engine.

Liverpool & Manchester Railway 0-2-2 locomotive *Rocket*
The sectioned replica of *Rocket* was built in 1934 for the Science Museum to show the design of firebox, boiler, cylinders and blastpipe.

London & South Western Railway 4-4-0 passenger locomotive No 563 (1893)
The 4-4-0 tender locomotive dominated passenger train working in the British Isles in the late nineteenth and early twentieth centuries. LSWR locomotive No 563 was designed to work fast, heavy, main line traffic, particularly on the Salisbury to Exeter line with its steep gradients.

London & South Western Railway 4-4-0 locomotive No 563, 1893

The development of the locomotive
Steam traction

Great Eastern Railway 0-6-0 locomotive No 1217 was built at Stratford Works, North London, in 1905 and remained in service until 1962

capabilities. Using four instead of six coupled wheels, however, meant a loss of adhesive weight and eventually the 4-6-0 and 4-6-2 arrangements gained wider acceptance.

The archetypal British goods locomotive was a simple six-wheeled design in which all wheels were coupled so that the entire weight of the locomotive was available for adhesion. The 0-6-0 came in all shapes and sizes and had many duties. North Eastern Railway No 1275 (1874) is an early example. As goods locomotives grew in size and became more powerful, 0-8-0, 2-8-0 and 2-10-0 wheel arrangements were used.

The tank engine, developed for short-distance passenger, goods and shunting work, did not need a separate tender as it carried its fuel and water supplies on the same main frame as the locomotive. Great Eastern Railway No 87 (1904) is an example of a passenger tank locomotive used successfully on the intensive suburban services to and from London's Liverpool Street station.

As speeds increased and train loads grew heavier, locomotives grew in size and many refinements were made to improve their efficiency and performance. Perhaps the biggest single aid to efficiency was the superheater devised by Wilhelm Schmidt in Germany and introduced to Britain in 1906. The superheater, increased the temperature of the steam produced by the boiler, making better use of its expansive power within the cylinders. This enabled locomotives to generate more power without using more fuel and without increasing the weight and complexity of the locomotive. Compound locomotives – which also produced a saving in fuel by using steam twice, first in one or more high pressure cylinders and then again in one or more low pressure cylinders – were never widely used in Britain. Their saving in coal consumption was outweighed by their greater complexity and the increased maintenance required. Midland Railway 4-4-0 No 1000 (1904) is an example of a three-cylinder compound locomotive.

In the early twentieth century, the Great Western Railway led the way in locomotive development. Its chief engineer, George Jackson Churchward, drew on French and American practice to produce advanced designs. No 4003, *Lode Star* (1907), is one of the first four-cylinder passenger locomotives, which, with their derivatives, set the standards for passenger work on the Great Western Railway until the 1930s.

Great Western Railway locomotives were among the most advanced in 1923 when more than 120 railway companies were grouped into four large ones. The London & North Eastern Railway, the London Midland & Scottish Railway and the Southern Railway all produced some outstanding locomotive designs to equal those of the Great Western. Nigel Gresley's three-cylinder locomotives for the LNER matured in the *Green Arrow* type (1936) and in the A4-class express passenger streamline locomotives of which *Mallard* No 4468 (1938) is a famous example. By the mid-1930s William Stanier for the LMS produced the class 5 mixed-traffic type locomotive of which No 5000 (1935) is the first and the Princess Coronation class which were among the most powerful express locomotives in Britain. The Southern Railway pioneered electrification but during the Second World War its chief mechanical engineer, Oliver Bulleid, produced an advanced steam locomotive design with a welded steel firebox (in place of copper). No 35029 *Ellerman Lines* (1949) survives as a rebuilt and sectioned example.

Between 1951 and 1960 British Railways built 999 steam locomotives of standard designs. All but one were two-cylinder locomotives for mixed-traffic or freight duties and were designed with ease of maintenance in mind. *Evening Star*, a 2-10-0 heavy freight locomotive of 1960, was the last steam locomotive built for British Railways.

Great Western Railway 4-6-0 locomotive No 4003, *Lode Star*, 1907

London & North Eastern Railway
4-6-2 locomotive No 4468, *Mallard*, 1938

In Perspective No 5 – The Locomotive was a poster produced by the London Midland & Scottish Railway in 1947

Things to see ...

The Great Hall
Great Eastern Railway 0-6-0 goods locomotive shown in its later livery as LNER 8217 (1905)
Goods locomotives required as much weight as possible on the driving wheels for adhesion, hence all six small-diameter wheels were coupled together.

Great Western Railway 4-6-0 passenger locomotive No 4003 *Lode Star* (1907)
Four-cylinder 4-6-0 locomotives were used extensively on the Great Western Railway. Most of the larger British passenger locomotives built subsequently had three or four cylinders.

London & North Eastern Railway 4-6-2 passenger locomotive No 4468 *Mallard* (1938)
Mallard holds the world speed record for steam traction of 126 mph. The record was set on 3 July 1938 in the course of trials on the brake equipment used in the coaches of the LNER streamline train *Coronation*.

British Railways 2-10-0 heavy freight locomotive No 92220 *Evening Star* (1960)
Evening Star was the last mainline steam locomotive built by British Railways. The use of 10 coupled wheels and an efficient boiler allowed improved haulage capacity at higher speeds.

British Railways 2-10-0 heavy freight locomotive No 92220, *Evening Star*, 1960

The development of the locomotive
Diesel traction

DIESEL locomotives, although more expensive to build, are more efficient in operation and cheaper to run than steam locomotives. All diesel locomotives have a diesel engine on board which burns fuel oil to provide the power which, via the transmission system, turns the wheels. In the British Railways Modernisation Plan published in 1955, the replacement of steam by diesel and electric locomotives was envisaged. Several diesel locomotive types were planned and many were supplied by Britain's private locomotive builders. D8000 (1958) represents the medium-powered units designed for freight work, while D200 (1958) is an example of express motive power. Both were built by the English Electric Company in their Vulcan Foundry Works, Newton-le-Willows.

The greater flexibility and availability for work of a diesel locomotive (its engine could simply be switched on, unlike a steam locomotive which required hours of preparation before it could be used) meant that the same level of service could be maintained with fewer locomotives. On the Edinburgh to Glasgow line 12 diesel locomotives replaced 30 steam locomotives. On the East Coast Main Line 218 diesel locomotives replaced 500 steam locomotives. Diesel and electric traction finally displaced steam in 1968.

Diesel locomotives had been used in Britain before 1955 but mainly for shunting purposes. The London Midland & Scottish Railway introduced two main-line diesel electric locomotives in 1947, Nos 10000 and 10001, and from the 1930s both the LMS and the Great Western Railway had made successful use of diesel railcars. On

British Railways class 08 diesel-electric shunter No 13079 was built at Darlington in 1954

the eve of the Modernisation Plan there were 456 diesels on British Railways and 179 diesel multiple units (DMUs). By 1968 that figure had grown to 4,326 diesel locomotives and 3,810 DMUs.

In 1972 the prototype High Speed Train was tested with No 41001 as one of the power cars. The HST or InterCity 125 proved to be the world's most successful diesel-electric train. It introduced a new pattern of passenger train operation using fixed-formation train sets, each comprising two power cars (one at each end) and a mix of first class, standard class and catering vehicles.

There are three main types of transmission equipment used on diesel locomotives: electric, mechanical and hydraulic. Electric transmission is the most widely used because it is reliable and enables a locomotive to run efficiently at speed. Mechanical transmission, involving gear wheels and a gear box, is relatively cheap and effective but limits performance at high speeds. It is used on some DMUs and on shunting locomotives where speed is not required. Hydraulic transmission, used on the Western Region of British Railways until 1977, was much lighter than electric transmission, so improving the power to weight ratio, but proved expensive to maintain. A modern form of hydraulic transmission is now used on the latest DMUs.

British Railways class 40 diesel-electric locomotive No D200 hauled express passenger trains between London Liverpool Street and Norwich

British Railways prototype High Speed Train power car, 1972

An InterCity 125 leaving York station, January 1985

Things to see ...

British Railways class 08 diesel-electric 0-6-0 No 13079 (1954)
This shunting locomotive is an early representative of the most numerous class of locomotive ever to run on British Railways. There were 1,193 built between 1952 and 1962 in five British Railways workshops.

English Electric *Deltic* **(1955)**
This is a prototype diesel locomotive built by the English Electric Company. It was loaned to British Railways and tested on express passenger trains. Following the success of this prototype, British Railways operated a further 22 similar locomotives for use on the London to Edinburgh main line.

The South Hall
British Railways class 40 diesel-electric 1 Co-Co 1, No D200 (1958)
D200 was the first main-line express passenger diesel-electric locomotive to enter service on British Railways as part of the 1955 Modernisation Plan.

The development of the locomotive
Electric traction

THE advantages of electric traction – clean, fast and relatively pollution free – were recognised by the City & South London deep-level tube railway in 1890. Unlike steam or diesel locomotives, electric locomotives do not generate their own power. They collect the electricity they need to operate either from overhead wires or from an additional, third rail. Electric locomotives therefore have a good power to weight ratio and good acceleration. At the beginning of the twentieth century competition from trams stimulated the main-line railways to electrify in suburban areas. The North Eastern Railway (NER) and the Lancashire & Yorkshire Railway led the field with the electrification of selected lines in 1904. The NER pioneered the use of locomotives using electric current taken from overhead wires. North Eastern Railway locomotive No 1 (1904) was used on the steep branch line to the River Tyne quays in Newcastle. In 1922 the NER proposed to electrify the main line between York and Newcastle but the plan was not implemented. The first complete main-line electrification for passenger and freight trains had to wait until 1954 when the Manchester, Sheffield and Wath line was electrified. Class EM1 electric No 26020 (1951) was one of the two types of locomotives used on this route.

In the 1920s and 1930s the Southern Railway, inheriting lines electrified by the London, Brighton & South Coast Railway and the London & South Western Railway, continued their electrification programmes and became the dominant user of electric traction. The equipment used direct current from a third rail at a low voltage, such as 650V. The stock developed was all of the multiple-unit type. LMS No 28249 of 1916, a former London & North Western Railway driving unit, and Southern Railway No 8143 (1925), part of a 4-SUB unit, are examples of this kind.

Widespread electrification came about as a result of the 1955 Modernisation Plan and, apart from the Southern

This London & North Western Railway electric motor coach was built by Metro-Cammell in Birmingham in 1916 with electrical equipment supplied by Oerlikon of Switzerland

Region, 25,000 volts alternating current (25kV AC) from overhead wires was the preferred method. Between 1959 and 1974 the West Coast Main Line between London, Birmingham, Liverpool, Manchester and Glasgow was electrified. No 84001 (1960) is typical of the first generation of 25kV electric locomotives. The East Coast Main Line between London, Peterborough, Doncaster, York, Newcastle and Edinburgh was completely electrified in 1991. Class 90 and 91 electric locomotives can be seen passing the Museum.

A feature of modern electric passenger train operation is to use fixed formations with the locomotive at one end and a specially designed guard's van with driving compartment at the other. The locomotive either pushes or pulls the train along while the driver sits in the leading vehicle. This method of operation, which in Britain was pioneered in Scotland on the line between Edinburgh and Glasgow, is now commonplace on both East and West Coast Main Lines and for all Gatwick Express services.

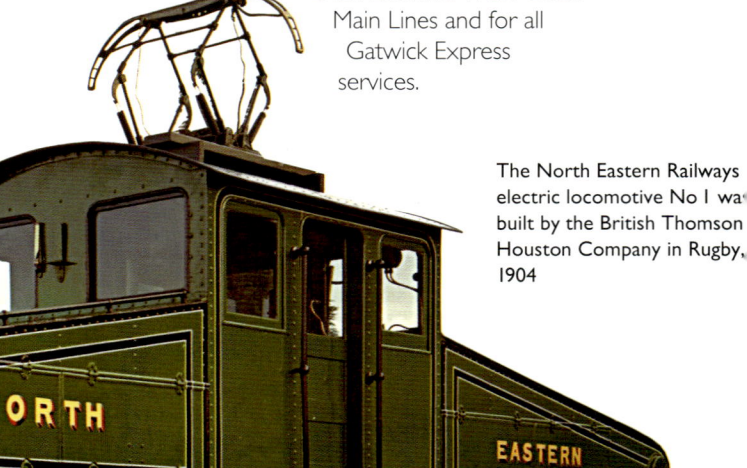

The North Eastern Railways electric locomotive No 1 was built by the British Thomson Houston Company in Rugby, 1904

British Railways electric locomotive No 26020 of 1951 although designed primarily for freight work was also fitted with steam boilers for train heating so that it could be used on passenger trains

EMUs leaving Guildford, 11 August 1939. On the left is a 4-SUB unit, in the centre, a train composed of two 4-COR units and on the right, a 2-BIL unit

British Railways electric locomotive No 84001 was built in Glasgow in 1960 and retired from service in 1979

Things to see...

The Great Hall

North Eastern Railway electric Bo-Bo No 1 (1904)
This was the first electric locomotive built for a British main line railway. It ran on the NER quayside branch line in Newcastle-upon-Tyne. The locomotive collected current from a third rail in the tunnel and from overhead wires in the open.

British Railways class EM1 electric Bo-Bo No 26020 (1951)
No 26020 was one of 58 freight locomotives built to work between Manchester, Sheffield and Wath on the first main line in Britain to be electrified for both passenger and freight operation.

The South Hall

London & North Western Railway electric motor coach (1916)
This electric motor coach is one of many designed for the North London Railway services from Broad Street to Richmond and the LNWR services from Euston to Watford. The NLR route was electrified by the LNWR in 1915 using direct current at 630V.

British Railways class 84 electric Bo-Bo No 84001 (1960)
The West Coast Main Line between London, Crewe, Carlisle and Glasgow was electrified between 1959 and 1974. No 84001 was one of the first generation of electric locomotives built for this service.

Locomotive servicing

THE site of the Great Hall of the Museum was once part of the York North locomotive sheds. The locomotive shed played a vital role in servicing and stabling its allocation of steam locomotives, and in preparing them for their turns of duty.

A large shed, like York North, which had an allocation of 150 locomotives, performed three major functions: first, the provision of coal and water; second, routine maintenance, undertaken about once every 10 days; and third, running repairs such as the replacement of valves, pistons and small boiler tubes. Major overhauls were undertaken at central works, such as Doncaster or Darlington, at pre-determined times or mileage intervals. When finishing a turn of duty, a locomotive was brought into the shed, its fire removed and all ash and char cleaned from the firebox and ashpan. The locomotive cooled down and its boiler was washed out to remove scale and impurities from the water. The boiler tubes were cleaned, the firebox carefully checked, worn parts were replaced and any routine adjustments and replacements of worn parts undertaken. Once this process was completed the locomotive was prepared with a fresh fire for its next turn of duty.

Fitter working on the London & North Eastern Railway locomotive, *Silver Fox*, at London, King's Cross, 1953

North Eastern Railway water column of 1920 shown filling a locomotive tender

The work of the motive power depot was overseen by the Shedmaster. Each shift had a foreman, and repair and maintenance were undertaken by skilled artisans such as boilersmiths. Firebar-boys, coalmen, labourers, cleaners and fire raisers attended to the routine needs of the locomotive on shed.

With the coming of diesel and electric traction the number of locomotive sheds decreased as locomotives were no longer needed in such large numbers. Fuelling and diesel maintenance were less labour-intensive. Today's sheds and depots are established and equipped to one of five levels of repair and overhaul.

The turntable built in 1954 by John Boyd and Co of Annan, Scotland is 70ft in diameter

Once the locomotive servicing was completed, the fire raiser went to work, 1936

Things to see ...

The Great Hall
The turntable (1954)
The turntable is still in its original position replacing a much older turntable. Capable of turning the largest locomotives such as *Mallard*, it was built by John Boyd and Co of Annan in 1954. It is still used for its intended purpose of turning and stabling locomotives and is occasionally demonstrated to visitors.

Water column, North Eastern Railway (1920)
Fed by a large tank or hydrant, a water column was used to fill a locomotive tender or tanks with water. Water columns like this one were found in locomotive sheds, on sidings and at stations.

The coal stack
This stack is modelled on the practice of the Great Eastern Railway and shows the tidy way in which coal was stored at the smallest of locomotive sheds.

The coaling stage at Huntingdon East on the Great Eastern Railway. Coal was transferred to the locomotive tender by hand

This poster by Terence Cuneo produced in 1946 shows an early morning scene inside Willesden shed

Cleaning out a locomotive firebox was a dirty and dusty job. A jet of water from a hosepipe was used to keep the dust down. Camden depot, 1955

Civil engineering and structures

RAILWAYS brought building and construction on a scale not previously seen in Britain. Neither the Romans with their roads and civic buildings nor the canal companies with their aqueducts and locks made such an impression on the British countryside as did the railway companies. Tunnels, cuttings, embankments, viaducts and bridges were built all over Britain. Large numbers of labourers, known as navvies, were employed, working under the supervision of contractors.

The station roof at York, January 1985. The station was designed by Thomas Prosser, Benjamin Burleigh and William Peachey and was opened in 1877

Constructing Kilsby Tunnel on the London & Birmingham Railway. From an illustration by J C Bourne, 1837

These men carried out the instructions of railway engineers such as George and Robert Stephenson and Isambard Kingdom Brunel.

To accommodate the limited capabilities of the early locomotives, the first railway lines had to be as nearly level as possible. The London & Birmingham Railway had no gradient more severe than 1 in 330. In consequence vast quantities of earth had to be moved and between 15,000 and 20,000 men employed. By the mid-1840s new techniques were being tried as locomotive power increased: the Lancaster & Carlisle line (1846) climbed Westmorland Fells with gradients of 1 in 75 over Shap Fell. Today, the high speed train in France, the TGV, can climb gradients of 1 in 28.

In towns and cities throughout the country, railway stations, hotels, and goods depots were built to serve passengers and other customers. Railway companies were strongly competitive and used their buildings to emphasise their authority and reliability. The heroic Doric Arch at Euston station (1837) proclaimed the London & Birmingham Railway as the gateway to the north while Brunel's Temple Meads station in Bristol (1841) with its hammer-beam roof suggested its continuity with the past. These early examples were later complemented by the majestic curve of York station (1877) and the exuberant Gothic architecture of the St Pancras station and hotel (1873), designed for the Midland Railway by Sir George Gilbert Scott.

The redevelopment of stations has continued to reflect the architecture of the times; the rebuilt Birmingham New Street (1967) is a purely functional concrete structure beneath a shopping centre; the new Manchester Airport and Waterloo International stations (1993 and 1994) use steel and glass in a late-twentieth-century echo of nineteenth-century practice.

To cross rivers and inlets bridges of stone, brick, wrought iron or steel were constructed. Robert Stephenson's tubular bridge across the Menai Straits (1849) and Fowler and Baker's massive steel cantilever structure of the Forth Bridge (1890) are impressive examples of railway additions to the landscape. Concrete was used for the first time in a major railway viaduct at Glenfinnan in 1898. To cut through hills, tunnels were bored. Kilsby Tunnel (1834–38) on the London & Birmingham Railway and Woodhead tunnel, built in two stages between Manchester and Sheffield (1839–45 and 1847–52), each required the labour of over a thousand men.

In this century the opportunities for large-scale railway building have been few and the engineers' efforts have been devoted to increasing capacity, providing for higher speeds and improving safety. However, the East Coast Main Line was diverted to avoid the Selby coalfield development in 1983. The principal railway project of the early 1990s has been the Channel Tunnel and its associated infrastructure.

The Gaunless Bridge spanned the river Gaunless on the Stockton & Darlington Railway, 1825

A North Eastern Railway footbridge from Percy Main station, 1891

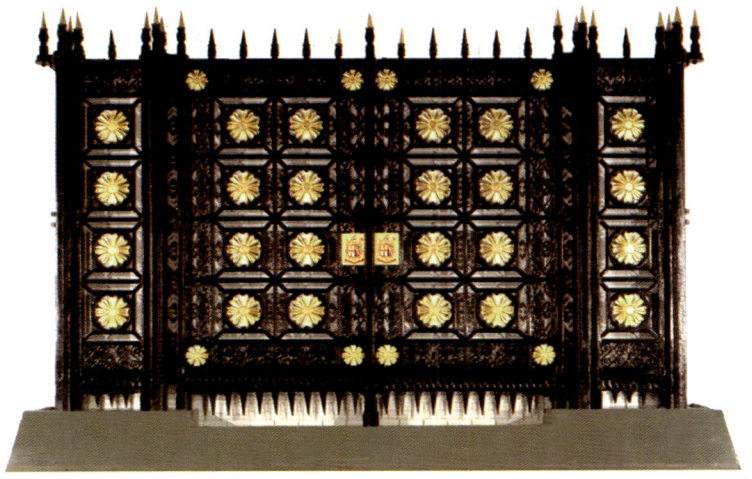

The Euston gates were manufactured by J J Bramah for the London & Birmingham Railway, 1838

Waterloo International station, 1993

The Forth Bridge, designed by John Fowler and Benjamin Baker, was opened in 1890

Things to see ...

Both halls of the Museum are former railway structures. The Great Hall, now substantially rebuilt, was a locomotive shed, and the South Hall was the North Eastern Railway goods station dating from the 1890s.

The Great Hall
Euston station gates (1838)
The elaborate cast iron gates were once within the enormous Doric Arch at Euston station.

The Gaunless Bridge (1823)
The Gaunless Bridge (by the Museum car park) is the first example of an iron railway bridge.

North Eastern Railway cast iron footbridge (1891)
A notable feature of many North Eastern Railway stations was the cast iron footbridge connecting adjacent platforms of double-track stations. The footbridge from Percy Main station near North Shields is typical of NER practice.

A short walk from the Museum are some railway buildings which are still in use:

● **York station** *(Queen Street)*
North Eastern Railway (1877)

● **The Royal York Hotel** *(on the south side of the station)*
Formerly the Royal Station Hotel (1878)

● **The original York station** *(in Tanner Row)*
York & North Midland & Great North of England Railway (1841)

● **The NER Headquarters and Offices** (1906)

Safety and signalling

THE railways' safety record is founded on a system of signalling which has evolved over the years.

In the earliest days of the passenger-carrying railway, hand or flag signals to stop or proceed were given to the drivers by railway policemen. The policeman in this role evolved into the signalman, who is still known to railwaymen as the 'bobby'. Signals at fixed positions were first introduced by the South Eastern Railway in 1841 and these, with arms to convey instructions to drivers, were the precursors of semaphore signals. In the earliest days, trains were allowed to proceed on a time-interval system. The signalman allowed a train past his signal post and then returned his signals to 'danger'. After a set time had elapsed the signals were cleared and the next train was allowed to pass at full speed. This afforded no protection to any preceding train that may have broken down or may have been slowed out of sight.

Interior of signalbox at Horsted Keynes, 1955

Display illustrating the operation of the ATC and AWS in-cab warning devices

In 1841 the development of the electric telegraph meant that signalmen could communicate with each other and trains could be passed from one signal post to the next. A space interval system of control replaced the time interval. This block system was designed to ensure that there was never any more than one train in any one section, or block, of track at any one time. Signals remained at 'danger' unless specifically cleared and the control of signals and track was centralised in signalboxes. The operation of signals and track was mechanically interlocked to prevent two trains being authorised to be on the same block at the same time.

Signal engineers have readily adopted advances in technology. Mechanical systems were masterpieces of logical thought and planning, but the application of science came early. Electricity was applied to signalling at the turn of the century; an electrically operated train detection device (track circuits), using a weak electric current in the rails, was introduced at King's Cross station, London, in 1894. The London & North Western Railway had an all-electric signalbox at Crewe by 1900. Colour light signals came into use in the 1920s and interlocking by electrical relays was introduced by the London & North Eastern Railway on the East Coast Main Line between Thirsk and Northallerton in the late 1930s. In 1937 the NX system (meaning entrance and exit) was introduced at Liverpool Brunswick station. This allowed the signalman to set up a path for a train on a panel by pressing switches at the start and finish of the required route – this route was then transmitted electrically to the track, operating and interlocking all the necessary points and signals. The system developed and was refined into the large power signalboxes of the 1970s in which the signalmen operated illuminated panels showing the positions and descriptions of trains and the aspects of the signals. Such signalboxes replaced many smaller ones and brought significant savings.

The Integrated Electronic Control Centre (IECC) now brings computer programming to signalling. Trains are dealt with according to a timetable in the computer memory. Routes are selected and set by the computer recognising the descriptive number of the train. The signalman interacts with the system not by lever or push button but by computer keyboard or trackerball; interlocking is commanded by the computer. At any time the signalman can override the predicted timetable if the service is out of sequence. An IECC can be much smaller than a power signalbox. Its computer system gives more flexibility as safety is inherent in the programmes, and the signalmen can concentrate on train regulation, ensuring a smooth and safe flow of traffic.

Section of Northolt signal gantry, 1942, in the Great Hall

Interior view of the power signalbox at York, 1989

Signal levers from one of the signalboxes at Garve on the former Highland Railway

The signalling gantry controlling the approaches to Blackpool Central station, 1921

Things to see ...

The Great Hall
The 'Signalling' exhibit in the Great Hall includes the following examples:

Semaphore and colour light signals
Operation of points interlocked with both semaphore and colour light signals.

In-cab warning devices
A signalling display which features in-cab warning devices for drivers, ATC (Automatic Train Control) and AWS (Automatic Warning System). AWS is the system in current use on Britain's railways. ATC was phased out in the 1970s.

Northolt signal gantry (1942)
A signal gantry of 11 lower quadrant signals from the Northolt Junction on the Great Western & Great Central joint line. The six yellow distant signals were worked by electric motor from the signalbox at Northolt Junction East. The five red stop signals were worked mechanically by lever and wire from Northolt Junction West.

The railways since 1955

WHEN the railways were nationalised in 1948 they were suffering from a lack of investment and a backlog of routine maintenance caused by the disruption of the Second World War. Steps had to be taken to improve and modernise the system. In 1955 British Railways announced its Modernisation Plan, which foresaw the gradual replacement of steam by diesel and electric traction and an improvement in railway services in response to increasing competition from road and air transport. In 1963, following continued financial losses, Dr Richard Beeching, the Chairman of the newly established British Railways Board, issued a report – *The Reshaping of British Railways*. This report called for a rationalisation of competing routes and a closure of over 2,000 stations. It also called for a modernisation of freight services and a move away from individual wagon loads to block trains of a single commodity which would reduce the time taken to assemble trains. The reduction in services and manpower became known as the 'Beeching Axe' and although matters were stabilised in the 1970s by the greater acceptance of railways as a social necessity, further proposals for reduction of mileage and services were made in 1983 in the unpublished Serpell Report. This envisaged a commercially profitable railway of about 1,600 miles based on a few major routes, but it was not implemented. The railway of 1994 retains about 11,000 route miles, half that in existence in the first years of the twentieth century when railways were at their zenith.

Against a background of difficulty in reaching a consistent transport policy, the railways have continued to develop. The Advanced Passenger Train, with its ability to run at increased speeds without major civil engineering work to realign the track, unfortunately faltered to a halt in the early 1980s. But the introduction of the InterCity 125 made a great leap forward in express passenger travel. Introduced in 1976 on the Paddington to Bristol and South Wales routes, this high-speed diesel train proved to be the world's fastest and in 1978 was introduced on the East Coast Main Line. Subsequently InterCity 125s have appeared on many non-electrified main lines. Electrification of the whole East Coast Main Line from London to Edinburgh was completed in 1991 and the HSTs moved on to other routes.

The late 1980s and early 1990s have seen the gradual replacement of the original Modernisation Plan diesel and electric units by modern stock. InterCity 225s on the East Coast Main Line, Sprinters on less dense routes and Networkers in the South are now an integral part of the much-improved railway scene. The formation, in 1968, of Passenger Transport Authorities (PTAs) promoted integration in public transport in urban areas. New stations were opened, old ones re-opened and urban light railways constructed in cities such as Manchester and Sheffield.

The railway of the 1980s and early 1990s also developed as a business-led organisation. Business sectors known as InterCity, Regional Railways and Railfreight Distribution replaced the former regions.

The 1993 Railways Act has broken up the structure of British Rail into a number of separate companies and franchises which, are now privately owned. The era of the publicly owned railway has gone.

The railways have been a fertile ground for the application of developing technology. Computers play an integral role in the railways and advanced techniques of design and maintenance have raised the reliability to high levels. New lines are represented by the Docklands Light Railway and the massive Channel Tunnel development with its associated infrastructures.

Railfreight depot plates from the Balcony Galleries display

Working on the East Coast Main Line overhead power lines, 1989

British Railways class 91 electric locomotive at York station, 1991

The Channel Tunnel, 1990 – building the British undersea crossover cavern which will enable trains to cross from one track to the other in cases of emergency or to enable maintenance work to be carried out

The Channel Tunnel is composed of two single-track rail tunnels, a ring of which is displayed in the Great Hall, and a service tunnel running between the rail tunnels

Things to see ...

The Great Hall
Railfreight depot plates (1988)
In 1982 British Rail was organised into a number of business-led divisions. Railfreight dealt with freight transport and each of its locomotives displayed a distinctive plate indicating the depot at which the locomotive was based.

Modern railway exhibition
The area near the Channel Tunnel in the Great Hall usually houses a display of equipment from the contemporary railway.

The Channel Tunnel (1992)
A ring of components from the Channel Tunnel is displayed in the Great Hall.

The East Coast Main Line runs past the Museum. The modern electrified railway can be seen through the north windows of the Great Hall.

Stratford terminal on the Docklands Light Railway, 1987

Narrow-gauge railways

Lynton & Barnstaple Railway coach, 1897

A narrow-gauge railway is one with its track gauge less than the standard gauge of 4ft 8½ins. As railways developed, narrow-gauge lines were constructed where the landscape or the potential traffic made the standard gauge physically impossible or an unattractive financial proposition. Narrow-gauge railways were much more adaptable than their standard-gauge counterparts – their curves could be sharper, and their earthworks and bridges of lighter construction.

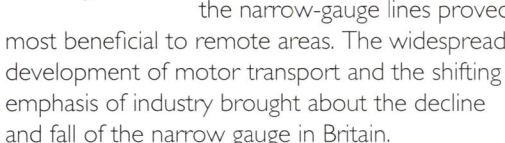

Poster for the Romney, Hythe and Dymchurch Railway, 1928

Most narrow-gauge lines were originally built for the conveyance of stone or minerals. The slate-quarry railways of North Wales and the lines serving the ironstone mines of Northamptonshire are good examples. Such railways were reminders of the earliest railway lines, running simply between a quarry and a port or main-line railway station. In the days before widespread road transport, the passenger service offered by the narrow-gauge lines proved most beneficial to remote areas. The widespread development of motor transport and the shifting emphasis of industry brought about the decline and fall of the narrow gauge in Britain.

Narrow-gauge lines came in varying sizes. The 3ft 6in gauge of Central and Southern Africa called for equipment which was often as large as much of that used on the standard gauge. Private locomotive builders such as Beyer, Peacock of Manchester perfected the articulated Garratt type of locomotive which combined power and flexibility on lighter track with sharper curves. Many of the private locomotive builders of Britain – Bagnalls of Stafford, North British of Glasgow and Hunslet of Leeds – once had flourishing order books to satisfy the needs of the narrow gauge world-wide.

The 3ft gauge lines of Ireland brought the benefits of transport to rural areas. None now survives, but in its day the County Donegal system was a model of efficient rural transport.

The Festiniog Railway (one of the first narrow-gauge railways) of 1ft 11½in gauge is one of the typical slate-quarry lines of North Wales. It was worked at first by gravity and horse power, from the quarries of Blaenau Ffestiniog to the sea at Porthmadog. In 1863 the Festiniog became the first public narrow-gauge line to use steam locomotives, and its trademark soon became the double-Fairlie locomotives which combined power and flexibility. In 1870 the Festiniog became the first user of bogie carriages in the British Isles. The Festiniog is now a fine example of railway preservation.

The minimum gauge for practical economic use is generally agreed to be 15ins. This arose out of the work of a Victorian gentleman engineer, Sir Arthur Heywood, who devised practical minimum-gauge railways for industrial, estate and military use. Unfortunately his work was overtaken by the advent of the internal combustion engine, but the 15in gauge became standard for small railways for fun. Today it flourishes as represented by the Ravenglass & Eskdale Railway and the Romney, Hythe & Dymchurch Railway.

The Tasmanian Railways Garratt locomotive of 1909 now being restored for the Welsh Highland Railway

The Festiniog Railway double-Fairlie locomotive *Livingston Thompson* of 1883 is on loan from the Festiniog Railway

Channel Tunnel construction locomotive and muck trucks, 1990

Things to see ...

The Great Hall

Festiniog Railway double-Fairlie locomotive *Livingston Thompson* (1883)
The second of the double-Fairlie locomotives of 1ft 11½in gauge built in the Festiniog Railway works at Boston Lodge.

Lancashire & Yorkshire 18ins gauge locomotive *Wren* (1887)
A number of these locomotives was used at Horwich Works. They delivered supplies, components and the weekly wage packets on the internal works system.

Lynton & Barnstaple Railway coach No 2 (1897)
The Lynton & Barnstaple coach spent much of its life as a garden shed and is shown here in this setting. It has not been restored but still gives some idea of the better type of passenger vehicle provided on the narrow gauge.

Channel Tunnel construction locomotive and wagon (1989)
These two 3ft gauge vehicles are a modern manifestation of the classic industrial narrow-gauge railway – rugged and functional. They were used in the construction of the Channel Tunnel. Lent by Eurotunnel.

Lancashire & Yorkshire Railway 18in gauge locomotive, *Wren*, 1887

Model railways

SINCE the 1830s and the widespread success of the steam locomotive, people have enjoyed toys based on railways. At first the early models were crude, but by the turn of the century firms such as Carette and Bing on the Continent and Basset-Lowke in Britain were bringing realism to model railways. Their models were first clockwork and then electrically powered. Two lines of development can be traced. Proprietary models such as those by Hornby, Triang, Bachmann and Rivarossi are commercially available. Those seeking a wider choice of prototype, combined with more accuracy, can build models from kits or commercially made parts or can create a complete model from raw materials. There are many scales and gauges and the modeller has a wide choice.

Larger locomotive and rolling stock models come in varying gauges from 2½ins to 7¼ins. Many of these models work by steam and are used by the Museum to show prototypes which are not in the National Collection. Visitors can ride behind one of the Museum's 7¼in gauge steam model locomotives such as *Margaret* (a North Wales quarry locomotive) or *Taw* (of the Lynton & Barnstaple Railway).

The Museum uses models to show many aspects of railway operation. Items made by railway apprentices as training exercises demonstrate the skills used and applied in the railway industry. Dioramas recall past events or buildings, and civil engineering models present, in manageable form, large structures such as bridges. Ancillary railway activities such as shipping are also represented in the Museum by makers' models, while model figures by Helen Mackie, whose work also included railway posters, give a representation of railway uniforms. To show specific aspects of railway operation, the Museum has built a model railway layout, St Paul's Road. St Paul's Road is an imaginary railway location, loosely based on Great Western Railway practice of the 1930s, designed to show a variety of trains in operation.

1:12 scale model built by E V Harrison in 1968 of the Great Western Railway 4-4-0 locomotive No 3440, *City of Truro*

These model figures were commissioned by British Railways from Helen Mackie in 1957

1:3 scale model of the Vale of Rheidol Railway 2-6-2 tank locomotive, *Owain Glyndwr*

Visitors enjoying a ride on the National Railway Museum's 7¼in gauge train hauled by the locomotive *Margaret*

1:12 scale model of the London, Brighton & South Coast Railway 4-6-4 tank locomotive No 333

The model railway layout of St Paul's Road was constructed in the Museum's workshop

Things to see ...

The Great Hall

London, Brighton & South Coast Railway 4-6-4 tank locomotive No 333, *Remembrance* (1974)
This 1:12 scale model of the London, Brighton & South Coast Railway locomotive No 333, *Remembrance*, was built by A L Perryman of Worthing between 1949 and 1974 as a memorial to the locomotives of the LBSCR. The model won the Crebbin Memorial Cup at the 1975 Model Engineering Exhibition in London. The original LBSCR locomotive No 333 was built in 1922 and named *Remembrance* in memory of the LBSCR employees who lost their lives during the First World War.

St Paul's Road model railway layout
The model electric railway in 7mm scale in the Great Hall features the train as the essential aspect of a working railway.

The South Hall

Vale of Rheidol Railway 2-6-2 tank locomotive *Owain Glyndwr* (1969)
This is a 7¼in gauge model built by Harry Powell in 1969 of the Vale of Rheidol Railway 2-6-2 tank locomotive *Owain Glyndwr* (1923). The National Railway Museum owns several 7¼in gauge locomotives, some of which operate in the South Yard giving rides to visitors.

Running the railways

FROM 1825 and the opening of the Stockton & Darlington Railway, the railway network grew rapidly. Each year new companies were formed and new lines built; by the eve of the grouping of the railways in 1923 there were over 120 private companies operating the railway system of the British Isles. Some of these companies, for example the Great Western Railway, were very large, with over 6,000 miles of track. Some, like the Southwold Railway in Suffolk, were narrow gauge and very short – a mere eight and a half miles.

The size of the railway operation and its workforce led to a need for detailed, efficient administration. The major example of successful large-scale organisation was the Army and the developing railway companies, like the canal companies of the eighteenth century, modelled many aspects of their administration on military lines. Chains of command were developed with the Chairman and Board of Directors at the top, the General Manager below them and the departmental heads such as the Chief Mechanical Engineer working to the General Manager. At the bottom of the chain and on the front line were the workers in the offices, on the platform and in the signalbox.

The companies created offices and administrative headquarters in keeping with their size and importance. The North Eastern Railway offices in York were described as a 'great palace of business'. Great advances in methods of administration, financial control and staff management were made by the railways, and many aspects of business administration today are founded upon the work of Victorian railway managers. The basis of discipline in the railway servants' employment was the Rule Book. Today this still forms the framework within which railway workers operate. It is further reinforced by the various health and safety regulations which together give railways an unparalleled safety record.

The matrices for the Common Seal of the Railway Clearing House, 1897–1963

Cash and wage bags for transporting money

As the railways grew and the companies ran joint lines and through services and exercised running powers on each other's tracks, so a system for standardising charges and apportioning revenue became necessary. In 1842 the Railway Clearing House (RCH) was formed to answer this need. The RCH apportioned revenue for through bookings involving more than one company. It established standard distances and rates for carriage of passengers and goods. It kept, from 1850, plans of all passenger and goods rolling stock and advised on standards, although it had no powers of enforcement. It settled inter-company financial disputes and oversaw the system of lost property within the railways. The RCH closed in 1963. The privatised railway system will once again need a clearing house to co-ordinate its operations and franchises.

The station master in his office at Edinburgh Waverley station, 1953

Train announcer at Edinburgh Waverley station, 1953

Calculating machine from the London, Brighton & South Coast Railway accountant's office in Brighton, 1879

Things to see ...

The Great Hall
The following are from the 'Running the Railways' display on the Balcony Galleries:

Cash bags
Cash bags were used for transporting staff wages from the Audit or Pay Office to local wages offices for distribution to staff.

Seals of Railway Clearing House
(1897–1963)
In 1897 the Railway Clearing House became a corporate body with a seal of incorporation.

Pencils, pens
No office was complete without a supply of pencils, pens, rulers, paper clips and other accessories, usually marked with the company's initials.

Calculating machines, slide rules and ready reckoners
Calculating machines helped with accounting and auditing in railway offices and made calculations quicker and less prone to human error. The railways have always been leaders in the use of such aids.

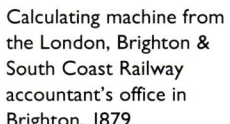
Guard's cap

Chief officers of the London & North Western Railway, 1910

Every railway company marked its property, including its pens and pencils, with its name or initials

25

Timetables and tickets

THE railway timetable is the means by which safe and complex train movements are organised. The published public timetable helps passengers to plan their journeys more efficiently.

The first timetables were handbills, posted or distributed at stations. As stations, routes and passengers became more numerous it was necessary to produce timetable books. A vast amount of work went into their production. Each train had its 'path' and the relation of that path to the paths of all other trains had to be most carefully considered. Whilst the timetable books for the individual railway companies fulfilled their needs, *Bradshaw's Monthly Railway Guide* contained the timetables of all the railway companies in Britain. George Bradshaw, a Manchester map-maker, produced *Bradshaw's Railway Timetable* in 1839. By 1842 this had evolved into the monthly guide. Essential to all who regularly travelled by train, *Bradshaw* endured until 1961 – only in the following year did British Railways produce an all-line timetable. *Bradshaw* is an example of a public timetable – the railways themselves ran to the *working timetable*. This covered all classes of train, goods and passengers alike. For special and additional movements, such as a royal train, a special train notice is issued.

Edmondson ticket dating presses used for validating railway tickets

The ticket office at Victoria station, London, 1950

The development of the railway timetable promoted the adoption of standard time. Even in a small country like Britain, time varied from east to west. This was not helpful to a railway company like the Great Western travelling due west from London to Bristol. By using the electric telegraph built beside the railway lines to communicate with stations and offices along their routes, the railways gradually adopted the time kept by the Greenwich Observatory in London as *railway time*. Only in 1880, however, did the Definition of Time Act make the use of Greenwich Mean Time a legal requirement throughout Great Britain.

Railway tickets act as a receipt, an accounting tool and a reminder to the passenger of his or her class of travel and destination. Initially the railways issued handwritten tickets in advance, or in the early days, asked for fares to be paid directly to the guard on arrival – a throwback to stage-coach practice. As trains, passengers and potential destinations became more numerous, a more flexible and quicker system was needed. This was developed by Thomas Edmondson of the Newcastle & Carlisle Railway in 1839. The Edmondson ticket was a pre-printed card measuring about 2ins x 1in, giving details for route and fare; it was validated by being date-stamped. Edmondson patented his system and for 100 years the booking office, with its racks of tickets and the 'thump' of the date-stamp machine, was an essential part of any station. Edmondson tickets came in all colours and served all functions – half-day excursions, workman, dog and bicycle tickets were added to the regular singles and returns.

By the 1950s and 1960s closures of stations and rapidly increasing fares rendered the Edmondson system outdated. British Railways began to use ticket machines which printed and validated tickets in the booking office and recorded the number and value of each ticket sold. Recent years have seen the adoption of computer technology in the form of APTIS (Accountancy and Passenger Ticketing Issuing System), its portable component (PORTIS) and credit-card-size tickets.

A selection of railway timetables

A selection of railway tickets

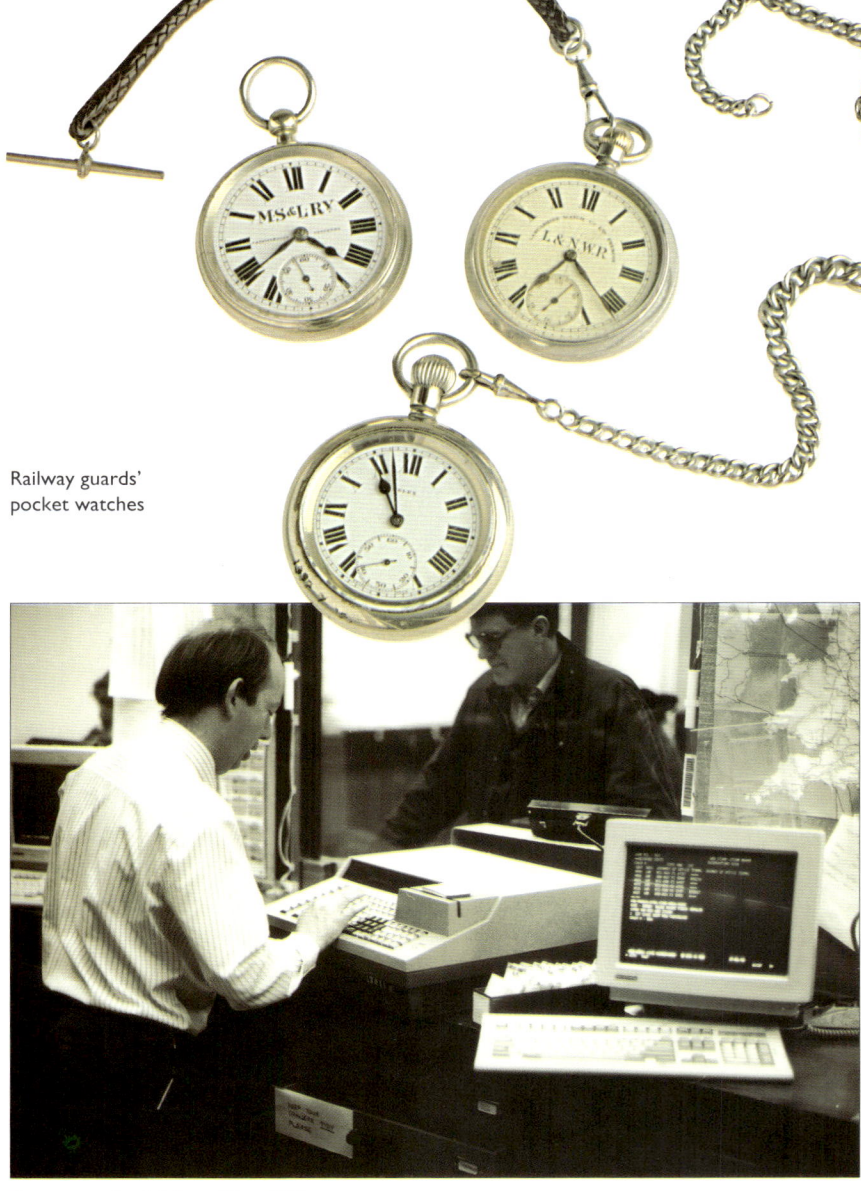

Railway guards' pocket watches

A computerised ticket office, 1993

Edmondson ticket printing machine, 1920

Things to see ...

The Great Hall
The following are from the 'Timetables and Tickets' exhibition on the Balcony Galleries:

Timetables
Timetables are produced and distributed for the information of the general public and for internal use by railway staff in many different forms.

Edmondson ticket printing machine (1920)
The major British railway companies had their own printing works. After nationalisation in 1948, British Railways concentrated all its Edmondson card-ticket printing first at Catlow Street, Euston, and after 1967 at Crewe. Modified Waterlow printing machines could produce more than 300 million tickets each year.

Clocks and watches
Accurate timekeeping was vital if timetables were to work efficiently, and this resulted in the production of railway timepieces of all shapes and sizes, from the pocket watch to the station clock.

Tickets
The use of coloured card for tickets was developed to help railway staff differentiate easily between classes of passengers. There were tickets for every passenger, including dogs, and for every occasion.

A complete service

THE principal business of the railways is to run trains and transport passengers and goods. The railway companies often saw no reason to allow others to profit from their efforts and so they branched out into other forms of business.

On-train services improved the style and environment of travelling throughout the nineteenth century. First came the introduction of heating and lighting, then corridor carriages with lavatories, and then sleeping and dining cars. Station platform refreshment trolleys were introduced and, for those passengers requiring overnight accommodation, sumptuous hotels were built at the larger stations: the Great Northern Hotel at King's Cross and the Royal Station Hotel at York are fine examples from the latter half of the last century. The era of the railway hotel ended in 1984 with the sale of The Queen's Hotel in Leeds to a private hotel chain.

The buffet trolley offering refreshments to Midland Railway travellers at Derby, 1908

Drew's *en route* tea basket, 1910, containing a kettle, burner, teapot, tea caddy and sugar bowl

Railway shipping also came to an end in 1984 when the British Rail shipping line, Sealink, was sold. The demise of railway shipping had been rapid, for even as late as the 1970s the British Railways Board owned 76 harbours with 95 miles of quay. The story of railway shipping goes back to the 1840s on the Clyde in conjunction with the services of the Glasgow, Paisley & Greenock Railway in 1841. By 1844 the South Eastern Railway was operating a cross-Channel service from Folkestone to Boulogne and in 1913, 216 railway-owned ships operated a network of services across the Irish Sea, the North Sea and the English Channel.

Particularly enterprising was the development, in 1933, by the Great Western Railway, of an air service between Cardiff, Torquay and Plymouth. In 1934 this became Railway Air Services, backed by the four principal railway companies. Railway Air Services operated internal routes and routes across to Ireland, and were joined in 1939 by Great Western and Southern Airlines. After the Second World War the railways' aeronautical interests were taken over by Imperial Airways, subsequently British European Airways.

The railways delivered passengers and goods to and from stations by horse-drawn vehicles. A door-to-door service was a valuable selling point. In 1903 the Great Western Railway offered motor bus services between Helston and the Lizard in Cornwall, and soon other companies such as the North Eastern and the London & South Western followed suit in their own areas. By 1928 the Great Western operated 330 buses on 154 routes but in the early 1930s, along with the other companies, these bus services were sold to solely road-orientated concerns and a great opportunity to develop a carefully integrated transport system was lost.

Camping coach advertising booklets

Relaxing during a camping coach holiday at Cheddar, 1956

Model of the diesel-powered ship, *Suffolk Ferry*, built in 1947, owned by the London & North Eastern Railway and then by British Railways

Paddle steamer *Waverley* leaving the pier at Rothesay on the Clyde coast, 1956

A Railway Air Services' aircraft at Speke airport, Liverpool, for the inauguration of the Liverpool to Plymouth service, 1934

London & South Western Railway horse ambulance, 1904

Things to see ...

The Great Hall
The following are from the 'A Complete Service' display on the Balcony Galleries:

Camping coach booklets
Camping coaches were placed on scenic branch lines with the aim of popularising holiday resorts that were not generally known and of encouraging rail travel.

Drew's *en route* tea basket
Drew's *en route* tea basket enabled the traveller to take refreshment at any time.

Suffolk Ferry (1947)
Suffolk Ferry carried freight trains between Harwich and Zeebrugge. It was owned by the London & North Eastern Railway and then by British Railways.

The South Hall
Road vehicles
The road vehicles display in the South Hall includes horse-drawn vehicles such as the Kent & East Sussex Railway horse-box and the London & South Western Railway horse ambulance – literally used to rescue 'broken-down' horses.

29

Locomotive and carriage construction

THE growth of the railways created a new flourishing industry of locomotive and carriage construction. The Forth Street Works of Robert Stephenson in Newcastle, opened in 1823, became the first builders independent of the railway companies; two years later the Stockton & Darlington Railway set up its own locomotive building works at New Shildon, Co Durham.

Throughout the steam age the larger railway companies built most of their own locomotives and carriages. Railway works formed considerable industrial enclaves in many towns, and over the years production ranged from the small (for example, the Inverness Works of the Highland Railway – 40 locomotives) to the massive (Crewe Works founded by the Grand Junction Railway – 7,300 locomotives over a period of 130 years).

The independent or private locomotive and carriage builders served overseas markets in Asia, South Africa, South America, Australia and, in the early part of the nineteenth century, North America and Europe, in addition to the railways at home. Firms such as Neilson, Dübs and Sharp Stewart in Glasgow, and Hunslet, Manning Wardle, Kitson and Hudswell in Leeds, were prominent amongst private locomotive builders. In Birmingham, Metro-Cammell and the Birmingham Carriage & Wagon Company produced passenger vehicles for export. Today the railway-building industry has greatly declined, with only a few private companies such as Asea-Brown Boveri (ABB) and GEC-Alsthom playing the major roles.

By the turn of the century the largest railway works were in the forefront of industrial development. The construction of a new type of locomotive took perhaps six months from concept to rolling-out, but existing designs could be turned out in a remarkably short time.

The record for the construction of a locomotive is 9 hours and 57 minutes, achieved by the Great Eastern Railway at Stratford Works, East London, in 1891. Normally a locomotive would take four to six weeks to build. The development of new locomotives started in the Traffic Committee, where the need for improved service was identified. The Chief Mechanical Engineer provided outline proposals for costing, approval by the Chief Engineer and financial approval. The Drawing Office then worked up the detailed design. Once the plans were drawn they were signed for by the Chief Draughtsman and the Chief Mechanical Engineer; the latter's name then became synonymous with the design. Thus locomotive designs were attributed to chief mechanical engineers such as Johnson, Wordsell, Churchward and Gresley.

The construction of locomotives and carriages brought together all types of industrial techniques. For locomotives, pattern making, casting, forging and coppersmithing were allied to the skills of the blacksmith, boilersmith and machinist. Similar skills were needed for the underframes of carriages, whilst the bodies were originally the province of the carpenters. Both carriages and locomotives spent some time in the paintshop before being passed into service. Today lighter materials such as aluminium and plastic are increasingly used in carriage construction, whilst the engineer is helped by computer-aided design. The end product remains the same – a safe and reliable vehicle.

A selection of works plates from the Balcony Galleries display

Working on a carriage at Wolverton Carriage & Wagon Works, 1933

British Railways 4-6-2 locomotive No 35029, *Ellerman Lines*, 1949

Gateshead locomotive works, 1910

1:8 scale model of a South Eastern & Chatham Railway open wagon, 1900. Part of the flooring has been removed to show the construction of the wooden underframe, buffing and drawgear

A poster design for the LMS by Lili Rethi depicting the construction of the Princess Coronation class locomotives at Crewe Works, 1937

Things to see ...

The Great Hall
Worksplates
Most vehicles in the Museum carry a pair of worksplates giving the date and place of construction.

British Railways 4-6-2 passenger locomotive No 35029 *Ellerman Lines* **(1949)**
Ellerman Lines was withdrawn from service on British Railways in 1966. In 1976 it was carefully sectioned on its right-hand side to reveal the internal construction and workings of a modern steam locomotive.

Balcony Galleries display
The display on the Balcony Galleries shows various components used in locomotive and carriage construction, and has a large number of models of locomotives, shown in chronological order to demonstrate development over the years.

The development of the railway carriage

THE first railway carriages were simple adaptations of the road stage-coach. Stage-coach-style bodies transferred easily to railway underframes and wheels, and the standard of comfort offered reflected stage-coach practice. 'Inside' on the stage-coach was to become 'first class' on the railway, 'outside' on the stage-coach was, initially, the spartan 'second' or 'third' class for the railway traveller of the 1830s. This theme of comfort according to the fare paid is one that still runs through rail travel.

Interior of Great Western Railway buffet car No 9631 of 1934

Aboard a compartment train, 1963

As railways developed, so did the demand for carriages of greater capacity. The stage-coach bodies developed into the familiar carriage compartments carried on underframes with four or six wheels. These larger vehicles were used well into the twentieth century but their rigidity meant that they could not be developed much beyond 50 feet length. Thus was introduced the bogie carriage, a longer vehicle with separate sets of wheels carried in trucks at each end which pivoted freely, relative to the carriage body. Bogie carriages were developed in the United States; the first main-line company to use them in Britain was the Midland Railway in 1874. On the narrow-gauge Festiniog Railway, bogie vehicles had appeared as early as 1870.

The Edwardian era saw the zenith of traditional carriage-building craftsmanship. Wood remained the traditional material for carriage bodies, with steel becoming more common for the underframes. The carriage body was adapted to serve various functions such as dining, sleeping and carrying the mail.

Between the wars, steel panelling replaced wood on carriage body sides and smoother profiles were achieved. After the nationalisation of the railways in 1948, there was an opportunity to standardise carriage stock across the nation's railways: 1951 saw the introduction of the British Railways Mark I carriage. Embodying the best of previous practice, the Mark I featured an all-steel body welded to a steel underframe. It formed the basis of development for the next decade.

In the 1960s British Railways engineers began to experiment with coaches of monocoque construction, with the underframe and body as a single unit. The first vehicle of this type, the prototype Mark II, was introduced in 1962 and the present Mark III and IV vehicles of today's trains evolved from it. Today lighter materials, such as aluminium, are used in carriage construction but the body shapes can still be adapted to serve such diverse functions as sleeping cars or electric multiple units for commuter service.

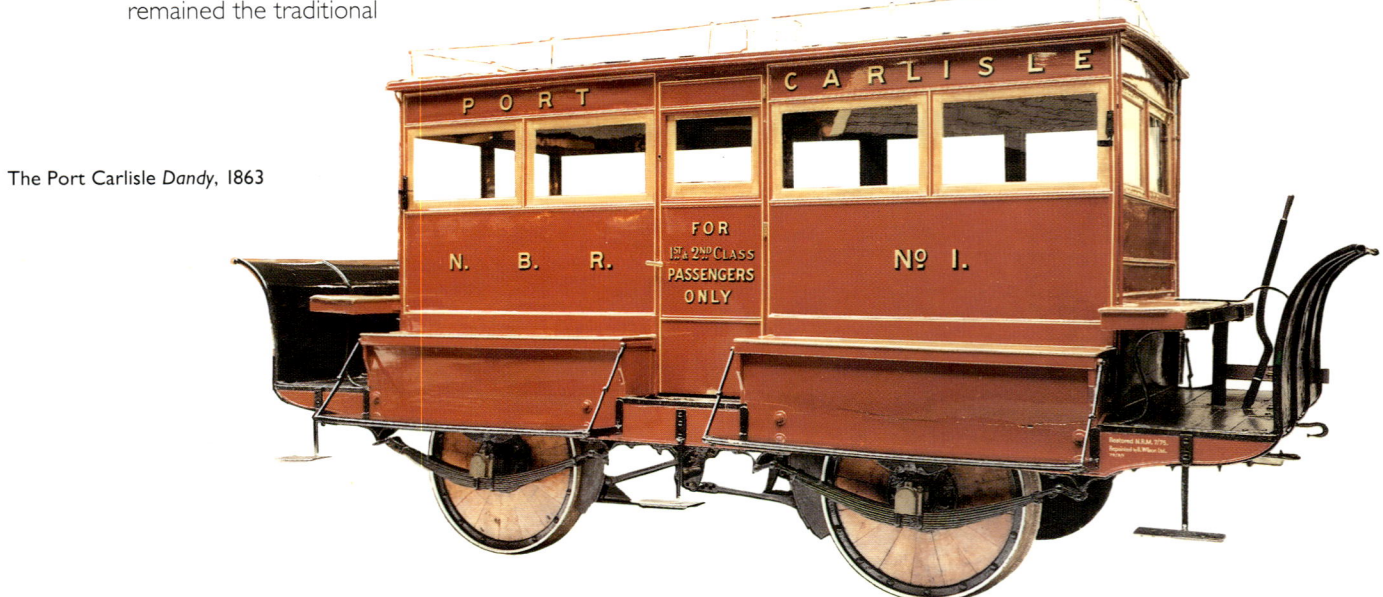

The Port Carlisle *Dandy*, 1863

East Coast Joint Stock third-class carriage, 1898

Stockton & Darlington Railway four-wheeled carriage, 1845

Things to see ...

The Great Hall

Port Carlisle *Dandy* (1863)
A direct link with the stage-coach, this 1 hp vehicle has passenger accommodation both inside and out, with luggage space on the roof. This vehicle is of very late construction for horse power and was used until 1914.

Great Western Railway buffet car No 9631 (1934)
This is a vehicle with steel underframe and panelling. Buffet cars were introduced by the Great Central Railway in 1899; they became very popular between the wars and feature on most InterCity trains today. This vehicle remained in use until the early 1960s.

The South Hall

Stockton & Darlington Railway four-wheeled composite carriage (1845)
Three stage-coach-style bodies on a railway underframe make a classic vehicle from the early days. The luggage space remains on the roof, as does a seat for the guard. One of his duties was to climb down when required and apply the brake to help to slow the train for station stops.

Great Northern Railway six-wheeled passenger brake van (1887)
A teak underframe carries a teak body. This vehicle was for passengers' luggage and the guard who operated the brake and was responsible for the safety of the train. Continuous automatic brakes for passenger trains were not legally required until 1889.

East Coast Joint Stock corridor third-class carriage (1898)
This vehicle has a steel underframe and teak body. The layout of a side corridor, compartments and a lavatory at each end of the vehicle followed a pattern established in the 1880s which continued into the 1970s.

Lifting a carriage body using a hydraulic lift at the Midland Railway Carriage Works, Derby, 1890

Great Northern Railway six-wheeled passenger brake van, 1887

Passenger travel

PASSENGER travel by steam train was so popular on the Liverpool & Manchester Railway when it opened on 15 September 1830 that the railway company delayed the introduction of its freight services until December to accommodate its eager passengers. The railways brought about a complete revolution in transport and introduced the concept of mass mobility: people could now travel about quickly, at least twice as fast as the stage-coach, in relative safety and in large numbers.

Passengers paid fares for first- or second-class travel, equating to 'inside' and 'outside' on the stage-coach. Third class appeared in 1838. In the earliest days, first class had a roof, windows and comfortable seats, and fares were calculated at about 2d (1p) per mile. Second-class passengers had hard seats and less space for about 1½d per mile, while the earliest third-class passengers frequently travelled in open vehicles with no seats. The Regulation of Railways Act of 1844 ruled that the railway companies must provide carriages with roofs for third-class passengers and that fares were to be fixed at 1d per mile; at least one train on each line each day must convey third-class passengers. These 'Parliamentary' trains, though frequently slow and inconvenient, brought about a significant increase in cheap travel.

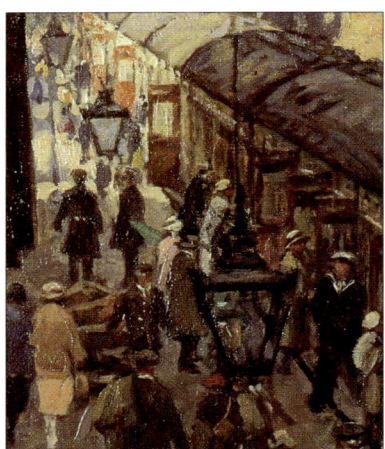

A busy scene at Penzance station – detail from the painting *The Terminus* by Stanhope Forbes, 1925

Passenger amenities improved slowly. Foot warmers, the earliest form of carriage heating, appeared in the 1850s. Heating was eventually provided by steam from the locomotive. Carriage lighting was by oil-lamps until the North London Railway introduced gas lighting in 1867. The first electrically lit carriages appeared in 1881 on the London, Brighton & South Coast Railway's elegant Pullman trains.

The North British Railway introduced the first sleeping-car service in Britain in 1873 and the Great Northern Railway the first dining car on its service between Leeds and London in 1879. In 1874 the Midland Railway introduced the first Pullman service into the country. Pullman cars take their name from the American, George Mortimer Pullman, who in 1859 introduced a superior type of carriage onto the American railroads. He provided services for passengers prepared to pay a supplementary fare, and developed a company which built and operated these superior carriages on the railroads of America. Other railways followed the Midland's example in England and Pullman cars were soon in operation all over the country. The *Brighton Belle*, an all-electric Pullman, marked the peak of service. Formal Pullman services ceased in Britain in 1967 and the Pullman Car Co ceased to operate. British Railways reintroduced the name and some elements of the service in the 1980s. Pullman Car Co vehicles were always distinctive; they carried a stylish corporate livery of umber and cream. First-class cars had names such as *Amethyst*, *Cambria*, *Stella* and *Doris*.

Dining cars, sleeping cars and lavatory carriages were advertised by the North British Railway on a 1907 poster

In Europe the Compagnie Internationale des Wagons-Lits et des Grands Express Européens introduced international sleeping-car services. Between 1936 and 1980 the *Night Ferry* was Britain's only international through train. Passengers travelled between London, Paris and Brussels without leaving their coach as the carriages themselves were carried across the Channel by train ferry.

A 1930 replica of an 1830 Liverpool & Manchester Railway first-class carriage

Going North, King's Cross station by George Earl, 1893

London Midland & Scottish Railway third-class sleeping car, 1928

Refreshments aboard *The Devon Belle*, 1953

Things to see ...

The Great Hall
Liverpool & Manchester Railway replica carriage (1930)
This is a replica of a first-class carriage built originally for the Liverpool & Manchester Railway in 1830. Although the seats for 18 passengers are padded, the simple leaf-spring suspension suggests an uncomfortable ride.

London Midland & Scottish Railway third-class sleeping car No 14241 (1928)
A carriage equipped both for day and night use, in conventional compartments served by a side corridor; each compartment can be converted to night use by four passengers.

The South Hall
Paintings by George Earl (1824–1908)
Going North, King's Cross station (1893)
Coming South, Perth station (1895)
The two oil paintings by George Earl depict the imminent departure by train of a shooting party and contain a wealth of contemporary detail.

Passenger travel

More general improvements to passenger comfort were instigated in 1875 when the Midland Railway abolished second class and conveyed third-class passengers on all its trains. First class remained very comfortable and third class was upgraded to equal second class. The Midland's was no philanthropic gesture; it was aimed at winning traffic from its rivals. In response other railway companies gradually followed suit and standards for passengers improved. The strange anomaly of the missing second class remained until 1956 when third class was renamed second. In 1987 second class as a designation finally disappeared when British Rail introduced standard class in its place.

British Railways poster, 1958

The railways capitalised on their ability to move large numbers of people quickly and easily. Whilst increasingly comfortable express trains covered long distances across the country, office and factory workers were daily conveyed to and from their places of work over relatively short distances. Many of the suburban railways were pioneers in the use of electric traction. The various underground railways in London developed rapidly from the 1890s; the Lancashire & Yorkshire Railway electrified lines on Merseyside and north Manchester between 1904 and 1916; and the North Eastern Railway operated a suburban electric system on North Tyneside from 1904. Later, in the inter-war years, the Southern Railway electrified many of its suburban routes. In this way the mobility conferred by the railways helped the growth of the major cities. The extension of the Metropolitan Railway services into the northern outskirts of London gave rise to the name 'Metroland' for the area.

At holiday times the railways moved thousands from the industrial cities to the seaside. Towns such as Clacton, Southend-on-Sea, Brighton, Blackpool and Scarborough received a considerable boost with the arrival of the railway. By the 1930s, passenger travel by rail was in its prime for business and pleasure. It was also for the first time in serious competition with road and even air travel. Famous expresses like *The Flying Scotsman* conveyed passengers to the north, and to win passengers in the 1930s this train provided a cocktail bar, hairdressing salon and cinema for its patrons. In the late 1930s streamline expresses such as *Silver Jubilee*, *West Riding Limited* and *Coronation Scot* brought main-line travel to new stylish heights. At the other end of the scale the branch-line train, often with its elderly locomotive and superannuated carriages, represented an endearing but slow and inefficient face of the railways.

In 1954 the first diesel multiple-unit trains went into regular service between Leeds and Bradford. Diesel and electric traction generally replaced steam but the greatest leap forward came with the electrification of the West Coast Main Line in the 1960s, and the introduction on the Western Region of the InterCity 125. This, the world's fastest diesel-electric train, became the flagship of British Rail and has subsequently been joined by a new generation of express passenger trains, the InterCity 225, hauled by the class 91 electric locomotives. On the cross-country and suburban lines a variety of modern diesel and electric multiple units have been introduced and are providing fast, air-conditioned comfort on a number of services.

A Southern Railway poster designed by Charles Pears in 1937 to advertise the electric services to Portsmouth, Southsea and the Isle of Wight

Awaiting the arrival of the train at Shenfield station, 1955

Things to see ...

The Great Hall
Southern Railway electric motor third brake No 8143 (1925)
A typical vehicle for suburban traffic. A non-corridor coach, it formed the front vehicle of an electric multiple unit.

The South Hall
Midland Railway express
The six-wheeled coach, No 901, dating from 1885, shows the improvements effected by the Midland Railway when it abolished second class.

The dining car, No 3463 (1914), shows both dining and catering areas to advantage. This vehicle was intended for third-class passengers.

Midland Railway third-class dining car, 1914

Southern Railway electric motor third brake, 1925

Delivering the goods

RAILWAYS were developed to carry minerals and freight. Wagon loads of coal, iron ore, limestone and other minerals travelled short distances on early railways to furnace, factory or waterway. With the coming of the steam locomotive, railways were able to carry goods in larger quantities and more quickly than existing forms of transport; they generated a second phase of the Industrial Revolution.

The railways specialised in bulk goods such as coal. They also carried all types of general merchandise and were obliged, by law, to be common carriers. This meant that they had to carry any load offered, be it as small as an egg or as large as an elephant. The requirement, finally removed in 1962, demanded much of the railways because road competition had no such obligations. The requirement was met by the 'pick-up' freight, a necessarily slow goods train stopping at every depot on a line, delivering and collecting loaded wagons at each one as required.

On the eve of the First World War the railways were carrying over 500 million tons of freight each year. This included virtually all of the items that industry and trade needed to move, from raw materials to the finished product, and from the commonplace to the bizarre. The railways carried many types of unusual goods: naval guns, ships' propellers, billiard balls and entire circuses, and for over 100 years two-thirds of all railway revenue came from the carriage of freight. Bulk goods, such as coal, coke and iron ore, travelled in trains of open wagons of 10 or 12 tons capacity. These trains were 'unfitted': the wagons had no brakes under the control of the driver, who had to use great skill in the use of the brakes on his locomotive. He also relied upon the skill of the guard in using the brakes on the brake van at the rear of the train. Valuable or perishable items such as vegetables, fish, newspapers, beer and milk travelled in covered vans or specially designed refrigerated or ventilated vans at higher speeds as 'fitted freight'. Such vehicles had brakes that worked from the locomotive.

After the First World War the release of thousands of ex-army lorries helped to establish the road haulage industry, and road competition bit into railway freight carriage. By 1938 only 263 million tons were carried by the railways, with coal accounting for 170 million tons. The Second World War accelerated the change. In the 1990s freight is carried at high speed in fully braked wagons and vans of high capacity or in containers which can be easily transferred to and from road haulage. Block trains, carrying one type of freight, are the norm but today the railways convey only 100 million tons of freight a year, 60 per cent of which is coal.

London Midland & Scottish glass-lined milk tank used by United Dairies, 1937

Road-rail containers were introduced to Britain during the 1920s

Great Western Railway 2-8-0 locomotive No 2818 heading a freight train through Honeybourne, Worcestershire, 1961

North Eastern Railway 0-6-0 locomotive No 1275 of 1874

Unloading horses at Ormskirk, Lancashire, 1914

Stanton Iron Company 12 ton mineral wagon, 1931

Things to see ...

The Great Hall
North Eastern Railway 0-6-0 No 1275
(1874)
The 0-6-0, with all the wheels coupled together, was the typical freight locomotive of the steam age. LNER No 8217 (1905) is another example, designed to pull trains of 750 tons at about 15 mph.

The South Hall
Great Western Railway 2-8-0 No 2818
(1905)
An outstanding type of freight locomotive designed for haulage of the heaviest coal trains from South Wales to London and of iron-ore trains from the Midlands to South Wales.

Freight wagons
● General freight: the freight train at platform 6 in the South Hall shows a representative selection of goods and minerals wagons. Note, especially, the coal wagon belonging to the Stanton Iron Company – a typical privately owned 12 ton mineral wagon.
● Special goods: the wagons are fully braked for conveyance of perishable goods at higher speeds. Note the insulated van for the carriage of bananas (BR 1960) and a glass-lined milk tank used by United Dairies (LMS 1937).

Royal travel

AS the railways developed, the larger private companies considered it extremely important to provide a special saloon for the reigning monarch. A handful of companies built entire trains. Impressive, purpose-built vehicles were provided for the royal entourage.

The locomotive and coaches for the royal train were always immaculately prepared, and each journey immaculately planned. These extracts from the special-train notice for Queen Victoria's journey between Holyhead and Windsor on Friday 27 April 1900 demonstrate:

> *3. A Pilot Engine ... will leave Holyhead Station fifteen minutes before the Royal Train and will precede it ... this interval is to be uniformly maintained throughout the journey.*
>
> *9. A 'Look-out Man' must be placed on the engine tender of the Royal Train, and must keep his face towards the rear of the Train, so as to observe any signal that may be given.*
>
> *25. All Level Crossings, Farm Crossings, intermediate Sidings at which there is no Signal Box, and all Stations must be specially guarded to prevent trespassers.*

Today precautions for royal journeys are rigorous but are as much concerned with security as with general safety of railway operation.

Queen Adelaide, widow of King William IV, travelled by train as early as 1840 but Queen Victoria was the first reigning monarch to do so. Her first railway journey was between Slough and London, Paddington, on 13 June 1842. Her Majesty pronounced herself 'quite charmed' by the experience, and thus set the seal of approval on railway travel. Queen Victoria's journeys to all parts of the country caused the railway companies to build a number of royal saloons for her, only one of which survives. This saloon, originally two vehicles, was built in 1869 by the London & North Western Railway. It was rebuilt as one vehicle and modernised in 1895. It is an elegant reminder of the height of Victorian style.

King Edward VII did not wish to use the vehicles built for his mother and no fewer than three new royal trains appeared in the early years of his reign. Those coaches built by the South Eastern & Chatham Railway have long since disappeared but the principal saloons of both the East and West Coast companies' trains are now in the Museum collections. The saloons built by the London & North Western Railway for King Edward VII and Queen Alexandra in 1902 and the East Coast companies' vehicles of 1908–09 are widely regarded as magnificent examples of the coach builders' art. King George V and Queen Mary used the Edwardian saloons throughout their reign.

The next royal saloons to be built appeared from the workshops of the London Midland & Scottish Railway in 1941. Reflecting a concern for war-time dangers, these coaches were designed to carry armour plate and served both King George VI and HM Queen Elizabeth II. They were finally retired in 1977 when new royal saloons based on the prototype Mark III coaches were provided. The Royal Family continues to use the railway for journeys around the country. The acceptance of former royal train vehicles into the Museum collection means that the National Railway Museum has the finest collection of historic royal carriages anywhere in the world.

Royal train headlamps

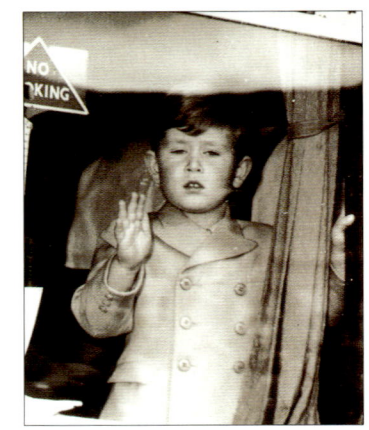

HRH Prince Charles waving from a carriage window before his train leaves Aberdeen for London, 1952

Queen Adelaide's saloon, 1840–42, was provided by the London and Birmingham Railway

The sitting room of the London Midland & Scottish Railway royal saloon No 799, 1941

Great Western Railway footwarmer from royal saloon, 1850–1901

The principal day compartment of HM Queen Victoria's saloon, 1869

The day room of HM King Edward VII's saloon, 1902

Talbot Road station, Blackpool, decorated for royal visit, July 1913

Things to see ...

The South Hall
Queen Adelaide's saloon (1840–42)
This delightful four-wheeled vehicle is the oldest with royal associations anywhere in the world. Built sometime in the period 1840–42, the coach includes a sleeping compartment and observation coupé as well as conventional accommodation. The coach was retired from service in 1847.

Queen Victoria's saloon (1869 and 1895)
The height of Victorian exuberance, this vehicle has patriotic interior décor in watered silk of red, white and blue. Originally two vehicles when built in 1869, the existing interiors were retained, at the Queen's request, when a single 12-wheeled underframe was provided in 1895. The interiors remain as they were last used by Queen Victoria in November 1900, a few weeks before her death.

The Edwardian royal saloons (1902)
Built at the Wolverton Works of the London & North Western Railway to the design of C A Park, these coaches are regarded by many as the finest example of railway carriage building ever achieved in Britain. They are displayed in LMS livery and with interior modifications made to suit King George V and Queen Mary. The dining car No 76 was originally a first-class vehicle of the West Coast Joint Stock which won a Grand Prix at the Paris Exhibition of 1900 before being taken into royal service.

London Midland & Scottish Railway royal saloon No 799 (1941)
The smooth outline and uncluttered interior of this saloon reflects the period of austerity in which it was built. From 1953 to 1977 this vehicle was Queen Elizabeth II's saloon. A similar vehicle, used latterly by Prince Philip, is loaned to and on display at the Transport Museum in Glasgow.

Mail by rail

THE speed and efficiency of the Royal Mail horse-drawn coaches in the early nineteenth century was legendary by contemporary standards but the coming of the iron horse gave a considerable edge in speed and reliability that the flesh-and-blood equivalent could not match.

The carriage of mail by railway began on the Liverpool & Manchester Railway on 11 November 1830. The General Post Office was quick to realise the potential of the new method of transport and sought powers from Parliament to gain control of mail by rail. Parliament did indeed give the Post Office considerable powers over the railways. It was empowered to put mail onto any train, but preferred to run special mail trains or mail trains with a single first-class coach attached.

The idea of sorting mail on the move had arisen in stage-coach days. It was a much more viable proposition on the railway and, in January 1838, the Grand Junction Railway introduced a Travelling Post Office – initially in a converted horse-box – between Birmingham and Warrington. The experiment was a success and the Post Office sorters greatly improved the efficiency of the service by travelling and working at the same time. It remained to develop a system of picking up and setting down the mails at stations without stopping and the first apparatus for this purpose was developed by Nathaniel Worsdell of the Grand Junction Railway in 1838. The Post Office did not buy Mr Worsdell's device but adapted a development of it, produced by John Ramsay, an employee of Missing Letter Branch, a year later. The final development of the apparatus, using nets rather than canvas chutes as in the first two types, was made in 1849 by John Dicker, another Post Office employee. It was this equipment that facilitated the development of an extensive system of Travelling Post Offices which at its peak comprised some 70 mail-carrying trains and about 160 specially constructed vehicles. One such train, the *West Coast Postal* travelling between London and Scotland, was the subject of the GPO film *Night Mail* in 1936. It took its name from the fact that all TPO services ran during the night. A classic documentary, this film featured an evocative poem by W H Auden as part of its commentary:

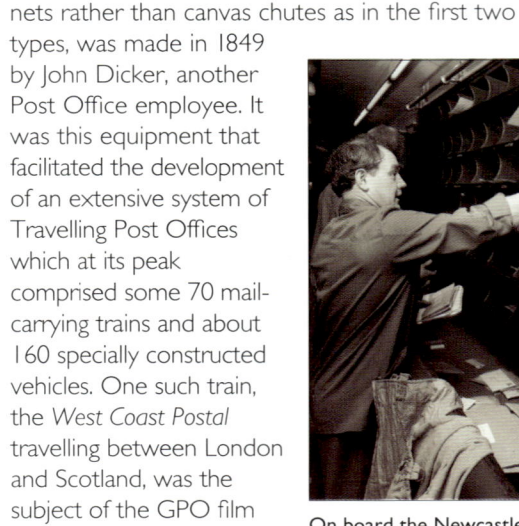

This is the night mail crossing the border
Bringing the cheque and the postal order ...

By the second half of the twentieth century less use was being made of pick-up and set-down apparatus. The last pick-up of mail on the move was made south of Penrith on 3 October 1971; from then on mail was brought by road to several principle stations and transferred to the Travelling Post Offices. In 1993 there were over 30 TPOs carrying all types of mail. In 1996 Royal Mail revolutionised its mail by rail operation with the introduction of Railnet. This saw new road to road and road to rail distribution centres at key locations around the country, new electric trains owned by Royal mail which stop at fewer places for less time and the gradual replacement of mail bags by plastic trays carried in wheeled containers.

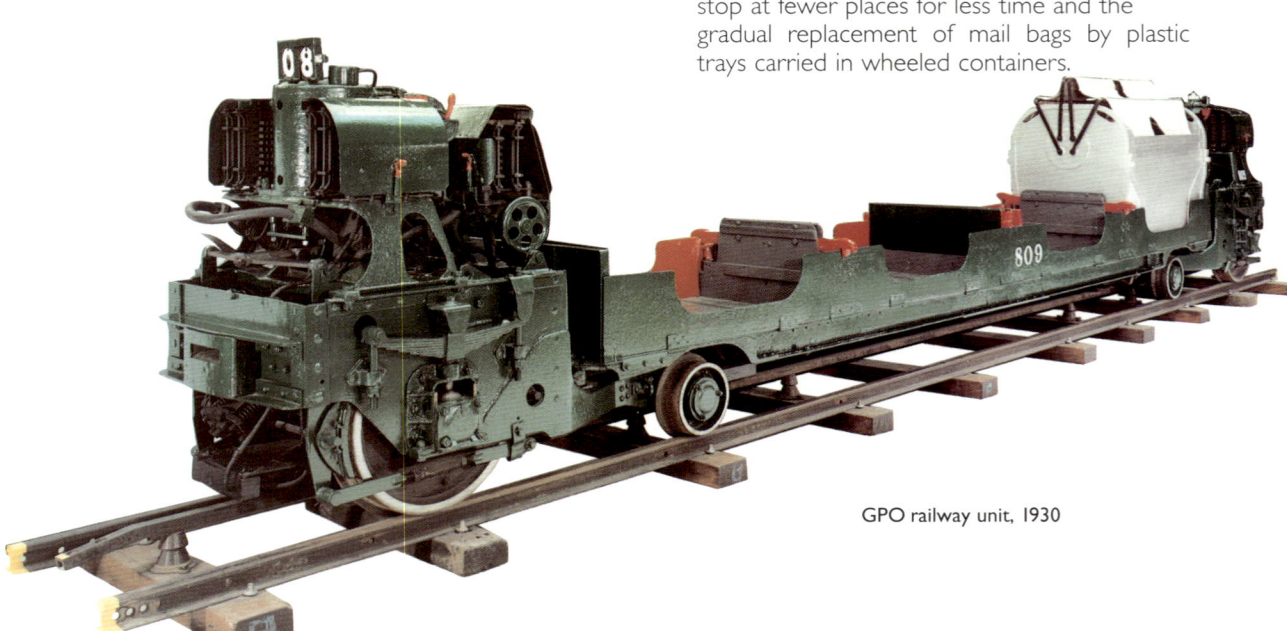

Pillar box from Sheffield Midland station, 1870

On board the Newcastle to London TPO, 1987

GPO railway unit, 1930

British Railways Royal Mail poster, 1952

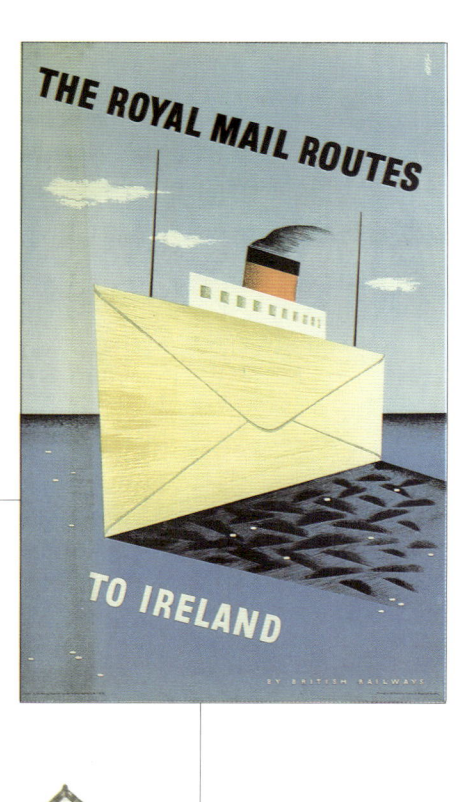

Mail bag being collected by TPO at Harrow West, Middlesex, 1957

West Coast Joint Stock Travelling Post Office, 1885

Things to see ...

The Great Hall
Moving Things - The Mail
An exhibition, which involves hands-on exhibits and a database, looking at how postal services have always used modern methods of transport, and particularly the railways, to ensure mail is delivered to its destination as quickly as possible.

The South Hall
GPO railway unit (1930)
This GPO unit is from the Post Office Railway which runs below the streets of London, connecting eight of the capital city's main postal centres. The units are driverless and run at speeds of up to 35 mph in the tunnel sections. They are automatically controlled.

Pillar box from Sheffield Midland station (1870)
This hexagonal pillar box was in use on platform 6 of Sheffield Midland station from 1870 to 1975. It is a working pillar box with daily collections; you are invited to use it for postcards and letters.

The railway workers

THE story of the railways is a story of people: millions of people who built, administered and operated the railways so that many more millions of people could use them for their daily needs of business and pleasure.

The first railway workers were the engineers and navvies. The engineers like George Stephenson, Joseph Locke and Isambard Kingdom Brunel drew up the plans; the muscle power of the navvies gave expression to those plans; major entrepreneurs, like George Hudson of York, and smaller shareholders provided the finance. By 1847 the railways had developed so rapidly that over 47,000 people were employed; by 1873 that figure had risen to 274,000.

The railways developed into some of the largest business organisations in the world; in the 1930s the London, Midland & Scottish Railway was the largest joint-stock company in the British Empire.

The railway offered secure employment with the prospect of advancement. It soon established a reputation for long service and loyalty. There was considerable pride in wearing the company's uniform although discipline was sometimes harsh, the hours long and the employees' conditions dominated by the Rule Book. It is hardly surprising that the railway workers strove at an early date for trade union recognition although it was not until the strike of 1911 that this was granted in any comprehensive form.

Advancement in the railway service was by a combination of experience, expertise and medical fitness. A signalman progressed by examination for increasingly complex signalbox operation. Booking office staff needed to be familiar with accounting procedures and needed to move about the system to achieve the rank of station master. In the footplate grades, a boy starting at 14 years old as a cleaner or firebar-boy might be 55 before he was the driver of a main-line passenger express; progress depended again on experience, medical fitness (especially eyesight) and a series of difficult practical and theoretical examinations.

The growth of the railway industry added to established towns or created new railway towns. Places like Derby (Midland Railway), Doncaster (Great Northern Railway) and Swindon (Great Western Railway) developed rapidly with the coming of railway junctions, offices and workshops; Swindon's population grew from 2,500 in 1841 to 45,000 in 1901. Towns like Crewe (London & North Western Railway) and Horwich (Lancashire & Yorkshire Railway) hardly existed before the coming of the railways.

Railway workers often gathered together in mutual improvement classes to add to their knowledge at their own expense and in their own time. Bands, ambulance units and sports teams were a feature. One such, the Newton Heath Locomotive Cricket and Athletic Club, has metamorphosed into today's Manchester United.

Until the First World War, railways were a largely male preserve. With the advent of the war, women took over jobs and rapidly proved themselves adept at what had been regarded as man's work. The Second World War reinforced this trend and today women are found in all walks of railway life. The nationalised British Railways employed a staff of 681,000 in 1948. Changes in working practices, increases in efficiency and the reduction of train mileage are such that in 1993 there are 122,000 railway workers.

London & North Western Railway locomotive footplate crew and pay clerks, 1860

The London Midland & Scottish Railway poster of 1946 indicated the variety of jobs carried out on the railway

Footplate of *Columbine*, 1845

Interior view of the London Midland & Scottish Railway brake van, 1933

Horse-drawn wagons at St Pancras station, 1912

Driver and fireman at work on the footplate of a Schools class locomotive, 1951

Two London & North Western Railway porters unloading luggage at Euston station watched by a higher ranking guard, 1906

Things to see ...

The Great Hall
The Wolverton Works Manager's office on the Balcony Galleries
The Works Manager at Wolverton Carriage Works near Milton Keynes oversaw the administration and day-to-day operation of the busy railway works.

The South Hall
Women on the Railways
The Women on the Railways exhibition looks at the contribution women have made to running the railways from the 1830s to the present.

London & North Western Railway 2-2-2 locomotive No 1868 *Columbine* (1845)
The early locomotives offered little protection to the driver and fireman from the weather.

London Midland & Scottish Railway brake van (1933)
The conditions for the guard were spartan.

Wolverton Works Manager's office as re-created on the Balcony Galleries

Museum services

A visit to the Museum is generally concerned with the exhibits in the two principal display halls. These displays represent only a part of the Museum's collections and activities and much essential work goes on out of public view.

The work of the Museum is concerned with the care and interpretation of the collections. Objects ranging in size from a locomotive to a uniform button are taken into the collections, catalogued, conserved, displayed, used for loans to other museums or made available for inspection by those engaged in research.

The Library and Archive Collections form the Museum's base for information and scholarly research. Appointments can be made to use the

The Museum shop

Reading Room where books, periodicals and learned papers may be consulted. The library holds a photographic archive of about one million negatives which cover all aspects of railway operation and come from official railway sources as well as from private photographers. Archival material on mechanical engineering is represented by a large collection of engineering drawings, locomotive test reports and history cards for individual locomotives. There is also a comprehensive collection of railway art – lithographs, paintings and posters.

The Museum's Education Service concerns itself largely with visiting school parties. The service operates 'Magician's Road' – a themed active-learning gallery where some of the principles of railway technology are explained. There is also a lecture theatre which is used for public film shows.

For further information on these or any other Museum activities, contact:
The Public Affairs Department,
National Railway Museum,
Leeman Road, York YO2 4XJ.
Telephone 01904 621261.

The Library Reading Room

Children enjoying a visit to Magician's Road

The National Museum of Science & Industry

THE National Railway Museum in York is part of the National Museum of Science & Industry.

The National Museum of Science & Industry is the world's pre-eminent museum devoted to the history of science, technology, industry and medicine. Its collections are the largest, the most comprehensive and the most significant anywhere. The core of these collections transcends in importance the purely national context; it celebrates the emergence of the first industrial nation and of modern scientific and industrial civilisation. The Museum serves its public at the Science Museum in London, the National Railway Museum in York and the National Museum of Photography, Film & Television in Bradford. The sheer size of the Museum's collections makes it impossible to display more than a proportion of them at any one time. Many items, including large vehicles and aircraft, are held at Wroughton in Wiltshire.

The Vickers Vimy aircraft flown by Alcock and Brown in 1919 on the first transatlantic flight is displayed in the Science Museum in London

The Science Museum collections of over half a million items embrace everything from an ancient calendrical sundial to Concorde, from medieval medical instruments to the model used by Francis Crick and James Watson to verify their ideas about DNA in 1953 and from astrolabes to the world's first patented animal, a genetically engineered 'onco-mouse' in 1989. The Museum has a long tradition of combining scholarship with interactive, visitor-operated demonstrations and exhibits. Launch Pad, opened in 1986, was Britain's first permanent interactive science centre. The 'hands-on' approach offers visitors – and in particular young people – a direct encounter with the worlds of science and technology.

For further information telephone (0171) 938 8000

The National Museum of Photography, Film & Television in the heart of Bradford's city centre

The National Museum of Photography, Film & Television collections include rare and illuminating material from every stage of photography's 150-year history, from the first images to modern cameras. In the television galleries, visitors can use TV cameras, experiment with vision mixing or try their skill as a newsreader. In the centre of the Museum is an IMAX big-screen cinema, the first of its kind in Britain. A regular programme of films is shown here and in the new Pictureville cinema which from 1993 has included Cinerama movies.

For further information telephone (01274) 727488

The open days at Wroughton attract many visitors to see the Science Museum's large exhibits which cannot be displayed in London

At Wroughton, near Swindon in Wiltshire, the Museum keeps the largest items in its collections, such as aeroplanes and heavy road vehicles. The site at Wroughton is open to visitors on selected weekends in the summer months.

For further information telephone (01793) 814466 or (0171) 938 8111

Index

Bold type: illustrations (usually in addition to textual references).

Adelaide, Queen, royal saloon **40**
Agenoria **4**, **5**
Air services 28, **29**
Atlantic type locomotives 6

Beeching, Dr Richard 18
Bradshaw, George, timetables 26
Bridges **14**, **15**
Brighton Belle 34
British Railways
    class 08 0-6-0 No 13079 **8**, **9**
    class 20 Bo-Bo No D8000 **8**
    class 40 1 Co-Co 1, No D200 **8**, **9**
    class 84 Bo-Bo No 84001 **10**, **11**
    class 90 and 91 10, **18**
    class EM1 Bo-Bo No 26020 **10**, **11**
    Deltic locomotives **1** (facing)
    Ellerman Lines 6, **30–31**
    Evening Star **6**, **7**
    High Speed Train (HST) 8, **9**, 18
    Modernisation Plan 8, 10, 18
    steam locomotives 6, **7**
Bus services 28

Camping coaches **28**, 29
Carriages 30–37
Channel Tunnel 14, 18, **19**, 21
City of Truro (model) 22
Civil engineering 14–15
Columbine **44**, 45
Construction
    of locomotives 30–31
    of railways 14–15

Darlington locomotive works 12.
Deltic locomotives **1** (facing)
Devon Belle, refreshments on **35**
Diesel locomotives 8–9, 18, 36
Dining cars 34, **37**
Docklands Light Railway 18, **19**
Duchess class locomotives 6

Earl, George, paintings **35**
East Coast Joint Stock carriage **33**
East Coast Main Line 10, 14, **18**, **19**
Edmondson, Thomas, tickets 26, **27**
Education service 46
Edward VII, King, royal saloon 40, **41**
Electric locomotives 10, **11**, 18
Electrification 10–11, 18, 36
Ellerman Lines 6, **30–31**
Euston station 14, **15**, **45**
Evening Star **6**, **7**

Fares 34
Festiniog Railway 20, 21, 32
Flying Scotsman, The 36
Forth Bridge 14, **15**
Freight services 4, **5**, 6, **7**, 18, **38–39**

Garratt locomotives 20, **21**
Gaunless Bridge 14, **15**
Goods services 4, **5**, 6, **7**, 18, **38–39**
Grand Junction Railway
    Columbine **44**, 45
    Travelling Post Office 42
Great Eastern Railway
    0-6-0 No 1217 **6**, 7
    0-6-0T No 87 6
    coaling stage **13**
Great Northern Railway
    4-2-2 No 1 **4**
    dining cars 34
    passenger brake van **33**
Great Western Railway 24
    2-8-0 No 2818 **38**, **39**
    air services 28
    buffet car **32**, **33**
    bus services 28
    City of Truro **23**
    handcrane No 537 **3**
    locomotive development 6
    Lode Star **6**, **7**
    signal gantry **17**
    timetabling 26

High Speed Trains (HST) 8, 18
Horse-drawn vehicles 28, **32**, **33**, **45**
    horse ambulance **29**
Horses, unloading **39**
Hotels 18, 28

Integrated Electronic Control Centre 16
InterCity 125s/225s 8, **9**, **18**, 36

King Edward VII, royal saloon 40, **41**
King's Cross station **35**

Lancashire & Yorkshire Railway
    electrification 10, 36
    Wren **21**
Library and Archive Collections 46
Liverpool & Manchester Railway
    first-class carriage **34**
    mail services 42
    passenger travel 34
    replica coach **34**, **35**
    Rocket **4**, 5
Livingston Thompson **21**
Lode Star **6**, 7
London & Birmingham Railway **14**, **15**
    royal saloon 40
London & North Eastern Railway
    0-6-0 No 8217 6, **7**, 39
    electrification 10
    Green Arrow 6
    Mallard 6, **7**
    signalling 16
    Suffolk Ferry **29**
London & North Western Railway
    Columbine **44**, 45
    electric motor coach No LMS 28249 **10**, **11**
    electrification **10**, **11**
    royal saloons 40, **41**
    signalling 16
London & South Western Railway
    4-4-0 No 563 **4**, **5**
    horse ambulance **29**
London, Brighton & South Coast Railway
    lighting 34
    Remembrance 23
London Midland & Scottish Railway
    brake van **45**
    diesel locomotives 8
    milk tanker **38**, 39
    royal saloons 40, **41**
    sleeping car No 14241 **35**
    steam locomotives 6
Lynton & Barnstaple Railway coach **20**, **21**

Magician's Road 46
Mail services 42–43
Mallard 6, **7**
Margaret 22, **23**
Midland Railway
    4-2-2 No 673 **1** (facing)
    4-4-0 No 1000 6
    bogie carriages 32
    Carriage Works **33**
    dining car No 3463 **37**
    first and third class travel 34, 36
    Pullman services 34
    six-wheeled coach No 901 **37**
    steel rails 2
Milk tanker **38**
Mining 2, **3**, 20, 38
    Agenoria **4**, **5**
Model figures 22
Model railways 22–23
Modernisation Plan 8, 10, 18
Motor bus services 28
Museum services 46–47

Narrow-gauge railways 20–21
Night Ferry 34
North British Railway, sleeping-cars 34
North Eastern Railway
    0-6-0 No 1275 6, **39**
    4-4-0 No 1621 **4**
    Bo-Bo No 1 **10**, **11**
    electrification 10, 36
    footbridge **15**
    water column **12**, **13**
NX signalling system 16

Owain Glyndwr (model) **22**, 23

Parliamentary trains 34
Passenger travel 34–37
Permanent way 2–3

Port Carlisle *Dandy* **32**, 33
Postal services 42–43
Pullman services 34

Queen Adelaide's saloon **40**, **41**
Queen Victoria's saloon 40, **41**

Rails **2**, **3**
Railway administration 24–25
Railway Air Services 28, **29**
Railway Clearing House (RCH) 24, 25
Railways Act 1993 18
Refreshment services 28, **29**, **32**, **33**, **34**, **35**
Remembrance (model) 23
Road vehicles 28, **29**
Rocket **4**, 5
Royal trains 40–41

Safety 16–17
St Paul's Road model railway 22, **23**
Servicing locomotives 12–13
Shipping 18, 28, **29**, 34
Signalling 16–17
Sleepers **2**, **3**
Sleeping-car services **34**, **35**
South Eastern & Chatham Railway
    4-4-0 No 737 4
    open wagon (model) **31**
South Eastern Railway 16, 28
Southern Railway
    electric motor coach No 8143 10, **37**
    electrification 10, 36
    locomotive development 6
Stanton Iron Company, mineral wagon **39**
Stations, building of 14
Steam locomotives 4–7
Stockton & Darlington Railway 2, **14**, 24, 30, **33**
Suffolk Ferry (model) **29**

Tasmanian Railways locomotive 20,
Tea basket 28, **29**
Timetables and tickets 26, **27**
Track circuiting 2, 16
Travelling Post Offices (TPOs) 42, **43**
Tunnels 14, 18, **19**, 21
Turntable **1** (facing), 12, **13**

Vale of Belvoir tramway **2**, **3**
Vale of Rheidol Railway 22, **23**
Victoria, Queen, royal saloon 40, **41**

Warning devices, in-cab 16, **17**
Water column **12**, **13**
Waterloo International station 14, **15**
Waterloo station **1**
Waverley, paddle steamer **29**
West Coast Main Line 10, **11**
West Coast Postal 42
Workers **3**, 12, **13**, 14, 44, **45**
Worksplates **30**, 31
Wren **21**

York station 9, **14**, **15**, 18

© Text and illustrations The Trustees of the Science Museum, 1994.

All rights reserved. No part of this publication may be reproduced or transmitted in any form or by any means, electronic or mechanical, including photocopy, recording or any information or retrieval system, without permission in writing from the publisher.

ISBN 1 872826 04 0

New colour photography by Paul Childs.

The National Railway Museum would like to thank the following for permission to reproduce illustrations: Terence Cuneo (*The Day Begins*, poster, p.13); QA Photos (Channel Tunnel photo, p.19); Aberdeen Journal (HRH Prince Charles photo, p.40).

Pictures in the guidebook are available for use through the Science & Society Picture Library, Science Museum, South Kensington, London SW7 2DD.
Tel 071–938 9749/9750/9752
Fax 071–938 9751.

Printed in Great Britain.